Knights of Consecration

Knights of Consecration

Dr. ant

Table of Contents

Knights of Consecration

Consecration to the Most Holy Trinity through the Blessed Virgin Mary

by

Dr. ant

Knights of Consecration: Consecration to the Most Holy Trinity through the Blessed Virgin Mary

Contents

Appendix A: Appendix

Additional Resources

Recommended Readings

Prayers and Hymns for Devotion

Introduction

In a world often overwhelmed by distraction and noise, the call to deeper spiritual life beckons with a serene yet insistent voice. For devout knights of the Knights of Columbus, this book intends to serve as both a lantern and a guidepost, illuminating the profound avenues of consecration to the Trinity through the loving intercession of the Blessed Virgin Mary. This introduction sets the stage for a transformative journey, one that leads to greater understanding and a more intimate relationship with the Divine.

The act of consecration is no mere ritual; it is a solemn and heartfelt commitment to live one's life under the mantle of divine grace. It is akin to entering a sacred covenant, where heaven and earth converge in the soul's sanctuary. For those with a devotion to the Blessed Mother, the journey toward consecration offers a pathway to the Holy Trinity that is both intimate and mystical.

The Virgin Mary, in her unparalleled humility and unwavering faith, provides the perfect model for consecration. Her yes to God's plan, the fiat that ushered in the Incarnation, is the ultimate act of surrender and trust. Through Mary, we learn to say our own yes to the mystery of Divine Love, embracing both its joys and its trials. This book will lead you through this journey, always drawing you closer to the heart of Mary, and from there, to the heart of the Trinity.

The Knights of Columbus, champions of charity, unity, and fraternity, have long understood the importance of Marian devotion. The order's commitment to the Blessed Mother is not just a testament of piety but an integral component of their spiritual and communal life. With Mary as their guide, the Knights find strength and inspiration to live out their vocations more fully.

Yet, to truly comprehend the depths of Marian consecration, we must first explore its origins and theological underpinnings. This journey begins by unpacking the concept itself, delving into its historical roots, and examining the lives of saints and scholars who have traversed this sacred path before us. Through their wisdom, we glimpse the richness and beauty of this spiritual practice, which now unfolds for us.

Understanding the Holy Trinity as a foundational aspect of our faith is vital. It's the mystery that stands at the heart of Christianity. By consecrating ourselves to the Trinity through Mary, we participate more fully in this divine mystery. The Blessed Virgin becomes our spiritual mother, leading us ever closer to Her Son and, through Him, to the Father and the Holy Spirit.

Throughout the sacred scriptures, Mary's role is foreshadowed and highlighted in the lives of various Biblical figures. From being the New Eve to the Ark of the Covenant, her typology is rich with meaning and significance. Each prefiguration brings us a step closer to comprehending her vital role in salvation history and illuminates our path toward consecration.

As we move through this book, you will be guided in cultivating a heart for consecration. It includes practical steps to develop a devotional life imbued with love and reverence. Daily practices, prayers, and reflections are shared to support your journey, creating a rhythm of life that continually draws you closer to the Divine.

Living in accordance with God's commandments and embracing His divine will require perpetual renewal and commitment. By aligning our lives with these truths, we open ourselves to the transformative grace of God. We become not just followers but active participants in His divine plan.

The virtues and natural law, concepts foundational to our understanding of morality and ethics, will also be dissected and examined. By grasping these principles, Knights can live out their consecration with clarity and purpose, embodying the values of charity, unity, and fraternity in every aspect of their lives.

Moreover, this book will explore pedagogical approaches tailored for the Knights of Columbus. It will provide insights on how to teach and reinforce the faith within the order, fostering a strong and vibrant community anchored in devotion.

Personal commitment and renewal of one's consecration are crucial. This involves not only understanding the importance but also learning the steps necessary to renew one's consecration. Each chapter builds towards this ultimate goal, preparing you for a life of dedication and devotion.

Understanding the duty of religion and how to seamlessly integrate it into daily life is essential for every Knight. This involves upholding the values and living according to the divine will, ensuring that one's actions always reflect a commitment to God.

Finally, this book presents original prayers of consecration, written to inspire and guide you. These prayers serve as heartfelt expressions of your love and commitment to the Blessed Mother and the Holy Trinity, encapsulating the essence of your spiritual journey.

This introduction serves as an invitation to embark on a journey of spiritual depth and transformation. The path is illuminated by the wisdom of saints, enriched by the virtues that guide us, and blessed by the maternal intercession of Mary. As you turn the pages, let your heart and soul be drawn ever closer to the Divine, and may your consecration be a testament of your unwavering faith and devotion.

Chapter 1: Understanding Consecration

Consecration, in its deepest essence, is a sacred dedication and an all-encompassing surrender to the divine will, an ardent commitment that transforms one's very existence into a living sacrifice. This profound act of consecration invites Knights of Columbus, and all Roman Catholics devoted to the Blessed Mother, into an intimate union with the Triune God through Mary, our spiritual Mother. It is through this spiritual journey that one's heart is moulded, refined, and led into the divine mysteries, echoing the timeless wisdom and allegories found within the Holy Scriptures. As we embark on this sacred path, we anchor ourselves in the historical tradition of Marian consecration, exquisitely intertwined with our faith, that has been illuminated by the lives and teachings of the saints. Within this sanctified relationship, the gracious influence of Mary guides us towards a profound and mystical communion with her Son, Jesus Christ, and the Most Holy Trinity, enveloping our knightly hearts with the virtues of charity, unity, and fraternity.

The Concept of Consecration

At the heart of Catholic spirituality lies the serene and profound act of consecration. Consecration is a word that carries within it the essence of commitment, dedication, and a deep-rooted act of surrender. It is the setting apart of oneself entirely for the service and glory of God. For the devoted, consecrating oneself through Mary to the Trinity embodies a special meaning, a unique spiritual journey that integrates divine love and eternal purpose.

Consecration is not merely an external act or a ritual; it is an internal, transformative process. When one consecrates himself to the Holy Trinity through Mary, it involves a complete giving of oneself—mind, body, and soul—to God. This commitment is as deep as it is broad, requiring not only a change in actions but also a profound transformation in one's very being. It's an act of love, loyalty, and devotion that transcends the mundane aspects of everyday life and touches the realms of the divine.

From the earliest days of Christianity, consecration has been seen as an embrace of holiness. In the light of Marian devotion, consecration takes on a maternal quality. Mary, the archetype of purity and obedience, guides her children through the pathway to sanctity. By consecrating oneself to Mary, the believer is taken under her protective mantle, leading them closer to the heart of her Son, Jesus Christ, and ultimately, to the Holy Trinity. This connection is not only inspirational but also deeply mystical.

To understand the concept of consecration, one must delve into the dual nature of its demands and promises. The demands are those of total fidelity and unwavering love. It is the call to live a life that mirrors the virtues of Mary—humility, chastity, and unwavering faith. These virtues become the foundation upon which the consecrated life is built. The promises, on the other hand, are those of divine assistance, grace, and an intimate union with God. The pathway may be fraught with challenges, but the spiritual rewards are immeasurable.

In the symbol-rich world of Catholicism, consecration stands as both an individual and communal act. For the Knights of Columbus, a fraternity bound by faith and devotion, consecration holds a particular significance. It is a commitment to live out their calling with renewed zest and purpose, one that aligns with their mission of charity, unity, and fraternity. Through communal consecration, they not only strengthen their personal faith but also fortify the collective spirit of their brotherhood.

The journey of consecration begins with knowledge and understanding. It is essential to comprehend what it means to set oneself apart for God, to be wholly devoted to His service. This understanding is the bedrock upon which the edifice of consecrated life is constructed. It involves studying the life of Mary, imbibing her virtues, and adopting her way of complete surrender to God's will. It is a spiritual apprenticeship under the guidance of our Holy Mother.

In the allegorical sense, consecration can be seen as a knight's quest. The knight, armed with faith and steeled by devotion, embarks on a journey through the spiritual realms. Guided by Mary, the epitome of heavenly grace, the knight moves closer to the Holy Trinity. Each act of devotion, each prayer, and each sacrament is a step on this divine quest, bringing the knight ever closer to celestial glory.

Consecration is also profoundly mystical. It is a moment where the temporal meets the eternal, where human frailty is engulfed by divine mercy. In this sacred act, the believer offers themselves wholly to God, trusting in His boundless love and mercy. It is a divine romance, an eternal union forged through the Immaculate Heart of Mary. This mystical union is not merely a lofty ideal but a lived reality for those who have traversed this path.

Moreover, the concept of consecration through Mary to the Holy Trinity emphasizes the mediating role of the Blessed Mother. Mary stands as the gateway, the mediator who intercedes on behalf of the faithful. Her role is to lead her children closer to Jesus and through Him, to the Father and the Holy Spirit. This mediating role is not an end in itself but a means to achieve the ultimate goal of divine union.

The call to consecration is a call to a higher form of living. It demands a sacred life, one that is in constant communion with God. This involves regular participation in the sacraments, daily prayer, and a life that reflects the virtues of Christ and Mary. It is an all-encompassing vocation that influences every facet of one's existence, from personal to professional life.

This call is also deeply personal. Each individual's journey of consecration is unique. While the communal aspect is vital, the personal commitment is where the heart of consecration lies. It requires a conscious decision, a heartfelt 'yes' to God's call. This personal agreement is the cornerstone upon which the grand structure of communal consecration is built.

However, the consecrated life is not without its challenges. It demands perseverance, patience, and above all, trust in God's providence. There will be moments of doubt, of spiritual dryness, but in these moments, the believer must hold firm to their commitment. The journey may be arduous, but the destination is divine union, a reward worth every trial.

In conclusion, the concept of consecration is a sublime integration of love, faith, and commitment. It is an act that transcends the mundane, reaching out to the divine. For the Knights of Columbus, it is a pathway to live out their calling with a renewed sense of purpose and devotion. Through Mary, they find a guide, a mother, and a mediator who leads them ever closer to the Holy Trinity. Consecration is the doorway that opens to a life of divine intimacy, a sacred journey that begins here and culminates in eternity.

Historical Origins of Marian Consecration

Our journey into understanding Marian Consecration must naturally begin by delving into its historical origins. The practice of consecrating oneself to Mary is deeply rooted in the early Christian tradition, emerging from centuries of deepening reflection on Mary's role in the divine plan of salvation. It is not merely a pious devotion but stems from theological developments and the lived experiences of the faithful over generations.

From the earliest days of the Church, Christians recognized Mary's unique position as the Mother of God. This foundational belief was cemented by the Council of Ephesus in 431 AD, where she was officially declared Theotokos, or God-bearer. This title reflected her essential role in the mystery of the Incarnation. Early Church Fathers, such as St. Irenaeus and St. Justin Martyr, were among the first to highlight Mary's significance in the salvation history, often drawing parallels between Mary and Eve. Just as Eve's disobedience brought sin into the world, Mary's obedience brought salvation through Jesus Christ.

In the Middle Ages, devotion to Mary blossomed further, given impetus by monastic communities. It was within these enclaves of prayerful life that the seeds of Marian consecration began to sprout. St. Bernard of Clairvaux, a 12th-century abbot and Doctor of the Church, extolled the virtues of Mary in his sermons and writings, emphasizing her as a powerful advocate and mediator. His teachings laid the groundwork for more personal and communal acts of consecration to Mary.

The flourishing of Marian devotion continued through the Renaissance and Reformation periods. It was in the 17th century that Marian consecration became formalized, largely through the works of St. Louis de Montfort. A French priest and missionary, Montfort authored the seminal work "True Devotion to Mary," wherein he expounded on the practice of consecrating oneself entirely to Jesus through Mary. He viewed this consecration as a complete entrustment to Mary, who would help form Christ within the soul, echoing how she bore Him physically. Montfort saw Mary as the most direct path to achieving union with Christ, and his method included rigorous preparation and a consecration formula that has endured through the ages.

While Montfort's influence cannot be overstated, the 19th and 20th centuries witnessed an extraordinary flowering of devotion to Mary, partly in response to numerous Marian apparitions approved by the Church. The apparitions of Lourdes, Fatima, and others highlighted Mary's maternal care for humanity and her call for repentance and consecration. These divine interventions further solidified the theology behind Marian consecration and drew millions to dedicate themselves more profoundly to her care.

A pivotal development in modern Marian consecration was introduced by St. Maximilian Kolbe, a Polish Franciscan friar who founded the Militia Immaculatae (Army of the Immaculate One) in 1917. Kolbe's approach to Marian consecration was shaped by his love for the Immaculate Heart of Mary and his desire to combat the spiritual and moral evils of his time. He envisioned consecration as a means of spiritual warfare, where the faithful consecrated themselves to Mary's Immaculate Heart to extend the Kingdom of God. Kolbe's profound insights into Mary's role as Mediatrix and Advocate inspired countless souls to join in his mission of total consecration and evangelization.

By the mid-20th century, the Church continued to deepen its understanding of Marian consecration, especially with the pontificate of St. John Paul II, who adopted "Totus Tuus" (Totally Yours) as his episcopal motto. This personal consecration to Mary, inspired by Montfort, underscored his belief in Mary's pivotal role in his spiritual life and mission. St. John Paul II spent much of his papacy promoting Marian devotion and consecration, particularly through his encyclical "Redemptoris Mater" (Mother of the Redeemer) and his establishment of the Marian Year in 1987-1988.

In contemporary times, the practice of Marian consecration continues to thrive. It has been embraced globally by millions of Catholics through various Marian movements and societies. The Legion of Mary, founded in 1921 by Servant of God Frank Duff, and the Family Rosary Crusade, initiated by Servant of God Patrick Peyton, are modern examples of how consecration to Mary can mobilize the faithful towards deeper prayer, evangelization, and service.

The historical trajectory of Marian consecration reveals a tapestry interwoven with theological reflection, mystical experience, and ecclesial endorsement. Each epoch has contributed unique insights, transforming Marian consecration from a devotional practice to a dynamic path of spiritual transformation. This history invites every Knight of Columbus and Marian devotee to grasp the profound heritage of consecration, viewing it not merely as an individual commitment but as a communal and ecclesial act that binds them more closely with the Church's mission and the salvific work of Christ.

Thus, the roots of Marian consecration extend deep into the Church's history, evolving through a synergy of theological insight, mystical tradition, and pastoral application. The practice stands as a testament to the enduring significance of Mary as not only the Mother of God but also as a mother to each member of the Church, guiding and shaping their spiritual journey towards the Trinity.

As we move forward in this exploration, let us carry with us the rich historical awareness that Marian consecration is not a modern invention but an ancient, living tradition that stretches back through the corridors of sacred history. Its origins give us confidence that our consecration today is part of an eternal, divine tapestry, intricately and lovingly woven by the hands of our Blessed Mother.

Chapter 2: Knights of Columbus and Marian Devotion

The Knights of Columbus, a brotherhood rooted in charity and unity, find a profound spiritual anchor in Marian devotion. This bond with the Blessed Mother transcends mere ritual; it blossoms into a transformative journey toward the Holy Trinity. As stalwart defenders of the faith, the Knights recognize Mary as the purest conduit to divine grace - a mystic rose leading souls to the heart of the Triune God. Their commitment to Marian devotion amplifies not as an obligation, but as a passionate call to embody her virtues: humility, obedience, and boundless love. By honoring Mary, the Knights fortify their spiritual armor, inviting her gentle guidance in every undertaking of charity and community service. Thus, Marian devotion emerges as the cornerstone of their consecration, not just enhancing their faith but illuminating the path to eternal truth and sanctity.

The Role of the Knights in the Church

The role of the Knights in the Church is not merely a badge of honor or a symbol of brotherhood. It is a solemn and profound commitment, woven into the very fabric of the Church's mission. The Knights of Columbus, as an esteemed fraternal organization, are more than just members; they are custodians of faith, guardians of tradition, and the Church's steadfast allies in the modern era.

Every Knight understands that his duty goes beyond the physical and the temporal. The Church, in her wisdom, has entrusted the Knights with the sacred task of being living witnesses to the Catholic faith. Their service embodies the values of charity, unity, and fraternity, which are fundamental to the gospel's teachings. The Knights are called to be the hands and feet of Christ, reaching out to the poor, the marginalized, and the downtrodden, thereby reflecting the Church's mission of love and compassion.

The Knights of Columbus play a pivotal role in upholding and disseminating the teachings of the Church. They spearhead initiatives that promote Catholic education, support seminarians, and aid those discerning priestly vocations. By fostering a culture of life, they stand against the tides of secularism that threaten the sanctity of life from conception to natural death. This unwavering commitment to the Church's teachings emboldens the laity to live out their faith courageously in a world often antagonistic to religious values.

Their role doesn't end at service but extends into the heart of the Church's spiritual life. Through their strong devotion to the Eucharist and Marian devotion, the Knights find the strength and grace to carry out their mission. Regular participation in the sacraments, especially the Holy Mass and Confession, fortifies them spiritually, enabling them to lead by example in their communities.

Moreover, the Knights of Columbus are instrumental in promoting Marian devotion, which is a cornerstone of their spiritual identity. By venerating Mary as the Mother of God and their spiritual mother, the Knights deepen their relationship with Christ. They understand that true devotion to Mary leads to a fuller and more profound consecration to the Holy Trinity. Through practices such as the Rosary, Marian consecrations, and feast day celebrations, the Knights foster a communal and personal devotion that unites them more closely to the Church.

The Knights' devotion to Mary isn't a mere formality; it reflects a heartfelt commitment to embodying her virtues of humility, obedience, and unwavering faith. In Mary, they find the perfect model of discipleship and an intercessor who continually leads them to her Son. This Marian devotion empowers the Knights to become better husbands, fathers, and servants of the Church, mirroring Mary's 'yes' to God's will in their daily lives.

The deep spiritual life of the Knights invigorates their commitment to serving the Church and her mission. They do not simply perform acts of charity; they do so with the full acknowledgment that they are extending Christ's love to the world. By serving the Church and the broader community, they become living icons of the virtues that the Church cherishes.

The Knights' role in the Church also encompasses a strong sense of fraternity and unity. By gathering together for regular meetings, spiritual retreats, and social events, they foster a sense of brotherhood that transcends individual parishes and communities. This unity is not just social but deeply spiritual, reinforcing their collective mission to uphold the Church's teachings and to evangelize through their lives and actions.

In addition to their charitable works and communal efforts, the Knights of Columbus uphold the Church's social teachings in the public sphere. They are vocal advocates for religious liberty, social justice, and moral values. Their voice serves as a testament to the Church's enduring influence in shaping a society that respects human dignity and the common good. By participating in pro-life marches, supporting family values, and advocating for ethical policies, the Knights act as the moral compass in a rapidly changing world.

Education and formation also constitute a vital part of the Knights' role in the Church. They organize catechetical programs, Bible studies, and faith formation sessions that deepen the understanding and commitment of their members and the wider Catholic community. By equipping themselves with knowledge and spiritual wisdom, they become effective evangelizers, ready to defend the faith and share the gospel with clarity and conviction.

The Knights of Columbus also play a transformative role in parish life. They are often the pillars of their parishes, supporting the clergy, participating in liturgical ministries, and ensuring the smooth running of parish activities. Their visible presence and active participation greatly enhance the spiritual and communal life of the parish, making the Church a vibrant and welcoming place for all.

To summarize, the role of the Knights in the Church is multifaceted and profoundly impactful. They are more than a fraternal organization; they are the Church's champions, dedicated to living out their faith in every aspect of their lives. Through their devotion to Mary, their commitment to the sacraments, their charitable works, and their advocacy for the Church's teachings, they embody what it means to be true disciples of Christ. As they continue to serve and lead within the Church, the Knights of Columbus ensure that the flame of faith burns brightly for generations to come.

Commitment to Marian Devotion

The Knights of Columbus, since its founding, has been a beacon of faith, unity, and charity. Integral to its mission is a deep and abiding commitment to Marian devotion. This devotion to the Blessed Mother is not merely an added spiritual practice but a reflective whole that enriches the Knights' lives and the wider Catholic community. This commitment represents a profound understanding of Mary's role in the economy of salvation and anchors the Knights to a spiritual tradition that spans centuries, drawing from the depths of the Church's wisdom and piety.

Being dedicated to Marian devotion means embracing Mary as the Mother of the Church, the spiritual Mother to all Christian faithful. Her maternal care and intercession create a spiritual haven, fostering a deeper relationship with Jesus Christ and the Holy Trinity. This commitment translates into the daily living out of Marian virtues—humility, obedience, charity, and purity—and offers the Knights a model of perfect discipleship. Through Mary, the Knights find a pathway to a more profound spirituality and a more ardent love for Christ, reflecting on how she magnifies the Lord through her life.

Within the Knights of Columbus, Marian devotion manifests in numerous ways, from public acts of reverence to private prayers and personal consecrations. Every Knight is called to not only honor Mary but to follow her example diligently. This involves a personal commitment to prayer, invoking Mary's intercession in all life's circumstances. The recitation of the Rosary, particularly, is a cherished tradition and a powerful devotional practice within the order. The Rosary, with its meditative rhythm and scriptural foundation, cultivates a deeper knowledge and love of Christ through the eyes of Mary, a perfect disciple.

Furthermore, Knights participate in Marian pilgrimages, feasts, and marathons of prayer, acknowledging Mary's pivotal role in the life of the Church. These communal activities not only strengthen individual faith but also foster solidarity and fraternity among Knights, uniting them in their shared veneration of the Mother of God. These gatherings are often occasions of grace, renewal, and evangelization, reinforcing the communal identity of the Knights as devoted sons of Mary.

The commitment to Marian devotion also involves educating others about the significance of Mary in salvation history. This educational mission is critical, particularly in a secular world that often overlooks or misunderstands Marian doctrines. Knights understand that by promoting such devotion, they are steering more souls to Christ, who is always found with His Mother. The teachings conveyed through various platforms—parish programs, seminars, publications, and digital media—aim to deepen the Marian spirituality of the faithful and encourage them to seek Mary's intercession in their personal journeys of faith.

Mary's role as intercessor, guide, and protector is a central theme in the Knights' devotion. Her own words in the Magnificat echo in the hearts of many, utterly transformed by the realization of God's work in their lives. It is through Mary's "yes" that the mystery of the Incarnation unfolded, making her the first and most faithful disciple. By emulating her total surrender to God's will, Knights rediscover the beauty of divine filiation and grow in their capacity to trust and obey the Lord, no matter how inscrutable His designs may appear.

A noteworthy expression of this commitment is the Marian consecration, often through the method popularized by St. Louis de Montfort. This consecration is a tangible and deliberate act of entrustment to Mary, reflecting a Knight's willingness to be led, shaped, and sanctified by her maternal care. Consecration to Mary is not the end, but rather a beginning—a continuous journey of living closer to Christ through, with, and in Mary. This spiritual undertaking requires preparation and a sincere dedication to grow in virtue and holiness.

Moreover, the Church has always recognized Mary's unique role in spiritual warfare. Knights of Columbus, aware of the spiritual battles they face in their lives and society, call upon Our Lady's intercession, knowing she has triumphed over the serpent. The prayer of the "Ave Maria" becomes a shield, a weapon, and a balm in the daily trials and tribulations. Knights walk confidently, knowing they are under the mantle of our Blessed Mother, protected and guided towards the ultimate victory in Christ.

Education on Marian devotion also encompasses the rich tapestry of Marian apparitions recognized by the Church. From Lourdes to Fatima, these heavenly visitations serve as reminders of Mary's ongoing involvement in the world's redemption. The Knights seek to understand and propagate the messages given by Mary in these apparitions, emphasizing conversion, penance, and prayer. Each approved apparition adds a layer to the Knights' devotion, offering both a historical and mystical context for their spiritual journey.

The commitment to Marian devotion within the Knights of Columbus is not only historical but is continually evolving to meet the needs of contemporary society. As new challenges arise, the Knights look to Mary for guidance and inspiration, ensuring that the devotion remains relevant and spiritually enriching. The precepts of Marian devotion—an intimate relationship with God, purity of heart, social justice, and unwavering faith—find application in the Knight's duties as Christians, family members, and citizens.

In conclusion, the Knights' commitment to Marian devotion is a multifaceted gem, reflecting various dimensions of spiritual life and service. This devotion fortifies the Knights' identity, enriching their faith and fostering a deep sense of community and mission. As they navigate the ever-changing currents of modern life, Knights find an anchor and a compass in their Blessed Mother, whose perpetual "yes" to God's will serves as an unfailing beacon of hope and love. Ultimately, the Marian devotion within the Knights of Columbus is a journey of drawing closer to Christ, through the loving and immaculate heart of His mother, Mary.

Chapter 3: The Trinity and Marian Consecration

In contemplating the profound mystery of the Most Holy Trinity, we find ourselves inevitably led to the gentle yet compelling guidance of the Blessed Mother, who acts as our pathway to divine communion. Through Marian consecration, we embrace a sanctified journey where Mary, full of grace, illuminates our understanding of the Father, the Son, and the Holy Spirit. In her immaculate heart, she mirrors the wondrous unity of the Trinity, helping us to deepen our relationship with God. As the Knights of Columbus, we are called to this sacred commitment, where Mary's intercession not only fortifies our devotion but also aligns us intricately with the very essence of Trinitarian love. Thus, consecrating ourselves to Mary isn't a mere act of pious devotion; it is our most profound step towards enveloping our souls in the divine mystery and love that binds the Three in One.

Understanding the Most Holy Trinity

In the grand symphony of cosmic events, the concept of the Most Holy Trinity stands as the most profound and mystical tenet of our faith. It is a divine paradox, a holy enigma composed of three distinct Persons in one singular essence: the Father, the Son, and the Holy Ghost. For centuries, theologians and saints alike have grappled with this mystery, each offering a prism through which the light of divine truth refracts. As Knights of Columbus devoted to the Blessed Mother, our journey towards consecration must begin with an earnest contemplation and understanding of the Trinity.

Imagine, if you will, the Trinity as an eternal dance, a perichoresis, as the Greek Fathers called it—a swirling, harmonious embrace of love and unity. Within this divine dance, the Father, the Creator, initiates the steps. It is He who speaks the Word, and through this Word, all creation springs into being. The Son, eternally begotten of the Father, consubstantial and coeternal with Him, is both the manifestation and the medium of the Father's intent. And then, from their infinite and reciprocal outpour of love proceeds the Holy Ghost, the Sanctifier, who breathes life, grace, and sanctity into the Church and souls.

The beauty of this Trinitarian relationship is not confined to metaphysical abstractions. It is enacted in history and made tangible through the Incarnation. When the Word became flesh in the person of Jesus Christ, the hidden divine life burst into the temporal world, making the mystical comprehensible. Here, the Son reveals the mystery of the Father and sends us the Holy Ghost, thus inviting humanity into the divine life.

Yet, our finite minds struggle to grasp this cosmic dance. How can one be three, and three be one? Analogies help but fall short. St. Patrick famously used the shamrock to illustrate the Trinity's unity and distinction. Others have likened it to the structure of an atom, with protons, neutrons, and electrons co-existing distinctly within a single atom. But even such images merely scratch the surface. The Trinity is ultimately a mystery to be embraced with faith, more than a puzzle to be solved with reason.

Within the mystery of the Trinity lies the mission of each Knight of Columbus. As warriors of faith, our task is to mirror this divine unity and love in our lives. Our consecration to the Trinity through the Blessed Mother is a solemn endeavor to participate more fully in this divine dance, both individually and collectively as an Order.

But why through Mary, you ask? Because Mary, in her humility and obedience, serves as the archetype of perfect devotion to the Trinity. As the chosen vessel through whom the Word became flesh, she reveals the Father's will, unveils the Son, and is overshadowed by the Holy Ghost. Her entire being is a testament to the Trinitarian life, making her the most fitting guide on our journey to deeper union with God.

In meditating on the Trinity, we also deepen our understanding of love, the very essence of God. St. John, the Beloved Apostle, tells us that "God is love" (1 John 4:8). This divine love is not static; it is a dynamic force that flows between the Father, Son, and Holy Ghost. It is this same love that we are called to emulate. Our acts of charity, our bonds of fraternity, and our commitment to unity within the Knights of Columbus are earthly reflections of the Trinitarian love.

Every prayer, every Mass, every act of devotion brings us closer to the Trinity. The Sacrament of the Eucharist, in particular, becomes a profound encounter with the Trinitarian life. In the Eucharist, the sacrifice of the Son brings us into communion with the Father and the outpouring of the Holy Ghost. This sacred mystery nourishes our souls and strengthens our commitment to live out our consecration.

The more we delve into the mystery of the Trinity, the more we realize that it is not an isolated doctrine but the very heart of our faith. It is woven into the fabric of our prayers, our sacraments, and our liturgy. The Sign of the Cross, with which we begin and end our prayers, is a simple yet profound invocation of the Trinity, reminding us of our divine heritage and mission.

In our quest to understand the Most Holy Trinity, let us not forget that it is ultimately about relationship—our relationship with God and with one another. As Knights, our fraternity is more than just camaraderie; it is a reflection of the divine unity. Our acts of charity are more than just good deeds; they are manifestations of divine love. Our commitment to unity goes beyond organizational solidarity; it is a testament to the one-ness of God in three Persons.

Thus, as we strive for deeper consecration through the Blessed Mother, let us continually turn our gaze toward the mystery of the Most Holy Trinity. Let this divine mystery inspire us to live lives of greater love, unity, and sanctity. For in understanding and participating in the Trinity, we find our ultimate purpose and the fulfillment of our mission as Knights of Columbus.

Mary as the Pathway to the Trinity

The mystery of the Holy Trinity forms the cornerstone of our faith, standing as the sublime union of the Father, the Son, and the Holy Spirit. To approach this divine mystery, we cannot overlook the pivotal role of Mary, the Blessed Mother. As we undertake the journey of Marian Consecration, it becomes clear that Mary illuminates the path to the Trinity itself, guiding us through her example and intercession.

Mary's fiat, her unwavering "yes" to God's will, sets the stage for her unique relationship with each Person of the Trinity. Her acceptance of the angel Gabriel's announcement showcases her complete openness to the Holy Spirit, her readiness to embrace the mission of becoming the Mother of the Son, and ultimately, her devotion to the will of the Father. This all-encompassing yes is not merely a one-time event but a continuous surrender to God's divine plan.

Consider the Annunciation, a moment when the angel Gabriel visits Mary with the news that she has been chosen to bear the Son of God. This encounter is more than an angelic visitation; it is an invitation into the intimate life of the Trinity. Mary accepts this invitation with humble obedience, becoming the Theotokos, the God-bearer. Through her, Jesus, the second Person of the Trinity, is incarnated. Thus, Mary stands at the very threshold of the divine mystery, facilitating our own entry into the life of the Trinity.

Imagine Mary's role in the life of Jesus. She nurtured Him, taught Him, and stood by Him throughout His ministry, up to the foot of the Cross. In doing so, she was not only a mother to Jesus but also became a model disciple, always pointing towards the Father. Her life mirrors her Son's mission to reveal the Father, making her a living pathway to understanding and loving God the Father through her relationship with Jesus.

Mary's presence at Pentecost further illuminates her role as the pathway to the Trinity. The apostles, gathered in the Upper Room, experienced the descent of the Holy Spirit while Mary was among them. Her presence underscores her unique relationship with the Holy Spirit, begun at the Annunciation and culminating in the birth of the Church. Through her continual intercession, she brings the faithful closer to the Holy Spirit, guiding us to live in accordance with His will.

In her apparitions, Mary has consistently directed the faithful towards a deeper relationship with the Trinity. Whether at Lourdes, Fatima, or Guadalupe, her messages consistently emphasize repentance, prayer, and a return to God's commandments. Through these appearances, she guides us back to her Son and through Him, to the Father and the Holy Spirit.

Mary's Immaculate Heart is a symbol of her perfect love and unity with the Trinity. Her heart, immaculately conceived and free from sin, reflects the purity and holiness required to approach the divine. Consecrating oneself to Mary's Immaculate Heart is, in essence, consecrating oneself to the Trinity, for her heart is the most perfect reflection of God's love and grace. Through her, we learn what it means to love God with all our heart, soul, mind, and strength.

Consider the Rosary, one of the most powerful Marian devotions. Each mystery of the Rosary points us towards the life of Christ and by extension, towards the Trinity. As we meditate on the Joyful, Sorrowful, Glorious, and Luminous Mysteries, we enter into the mysteries of Jesus' life, death, and resurrection. Mary guides our contemplation, turning our eyes towards her Son and inviting us into a deeper relationship with the Father and the Holy Spirit.

The Church Fathers and theologians have long emphasized Mary's role in salvation history as intimately connected with the Trinity. Saint Louis de Montfort, whose devotion to Mary has greatly influenced Marian Consecration, described her as the "mold" in which Christ was formed. To be shaped in this mold is to be formed in the image of Christ through Mary, thereby becoming more deeply united with the Trinity.

Mary's intercessory role cannot be overstated. At the Wedding at Cana, it was her intervention that led Jesus to perform His first miracle, revealing His divine nature. Today, she continues to intercede for us, bringing our needs and petitions before the throne of the Trinity. Through her motherly intercession, we gain access to divine grace and mercy.

The Knights of Columbus, with their deep commitment to Marian devotion, are especially called to understand and embrace Mary as the pathway to the Trinity. By following Mary's example and seeking her intercession, the Knights can draw closer to the Father, the Son, and the Holy Spirit. This journey is not just about personal sanctification but also about guiding others towards this divine communion.

In this sacred journey, the Eucharist holds a central place. Each Mass is a profound encounter with the Trinity, and Mary, as the Mother of the Eucharist, helps us to approach this mystery with a heart full of love and reverence. She leads us to the altar, where the sacrifice of her Son is made present, and through this sacrament, we are drawn into the eternal exchange of love that is the Holy Trinity.

In conclusion, as we continue our Marian Consecration, let us remember that Mary is our pathway to the Trinity. Through her example, intercession, and motherly love, she guides us into the heart of the divine mystery. By consecrating ourselves to her, we are consecrating ourselves to the Father, the Son, and the Holy Spirit, embracing the fullness of our faith and the depth of God's love.

Let us always seek to walk with Mary, our Blessed Mother, and through her, find our way to the Most Holy Trinity, the source of all grace, the center of our faith, and the ultimate goal of our spiritual journey.

Chapter 4: Typology of the Blessed Virgin Mary in the Bible

The unfolding tapestry of the Scriptures presents the Blessed Virgin Mary in profound typological splendor. In the gentle shadows of Eden, Mary's role as the New Eve resounds, for where the first Eve brought disobedience, she brings obedience and life through Christ. Consider her as the Ark of the Covenant, a pure vessel carrying the divine Word itself. Reflect, too, on her coronation as Queen of Heaven, exalted in majesty beside her Son. Throughout the Old Testament, she is prefigured by women of valor and grace — Sarah's faith, Esther's courage, the Maccabees Mother's enduring strength, and Judith's triumph — all point to her. In these images, the faith of our forebears finds fulfillment, echoing down the corridors of history to be venerated by the Knights of Columbus and all who devote themselves to her Immaculate Heart.

Mary as the New Eve

The notion of Mary as the New Eve is deeply embedded within the fabric of Catholic theology, presenting a profound typological connection that echoes through the ages. To grasp this, one must journey back to the dawn of time, to the Garden of Eden, where the original Eve dwelt in divine innocence before the fall of man. Scripture presents Eve as the "mother of all living," yet it is through her disobedience that sin entered the world. Her story is one of potential and failure, and it sets the stage for a future hope—a New Eve, one who would embody perfect obedience and bring forth new life.

Taken from this backdrop, Mary emerges as the New Eve in the pages of the New Testament. Where Eve's actions brought about a rift between humanity and God, Mary's "yes" to the angel Gabriel heralded the dawn of redemption. The contrast between Eve and Mary is stark yet beautifully complementary. Eve listened to the serpent and partook of the forbidden fruit, leading to the fall; Mary, on the other hand, received the Word of God through the angel's message and brought forth the fruit of her womb, Jesus Christ, the savior of the world.

In the Gospel of Luke, the Annunciation marks the pivot of this divine narrative. The angel Gabriel addresses Mary with the words, "Hail, full of grace, the Lord is with you." In her assent, Mary reverses Eve's disobedience. Here, in her fiat, or "let it be done unto me according to your word," echoes a cosmic restoration. Her acceptance ushers in a new dispensation of grace, where the obedience of Mary stands in stark opposition to the disobedience of Eve.

As Christ referred to himself as the New Adam, so too does tradition understand Mary as the New Eve. In his first letter to the Corinthians, Paul refers to Christ as the "last Adam" who became a life-giving spirit (1 Corinthians 15:45). If Adam, along with Eve, bequeathed death, Christ along with the New Eve, Mary, bequeaths life. This typology underscores the salvific partnership: just as man and woman brought about the fall, so too through a man and a woman comes redemption.

The early Church Fathers were quick to expound upon this typological relationship. St. Irenaeus of Lyon, in his seminal work "Against Heresies," wrote, "So the knot of Eve's disobedience was loosed by Mary's obedience." In this intricate tapestry of theology, Mary is seen as untying the knot of sin that Eve had woven, providing a direct line of continuity and contrast from Old Testament prophecy to New Testament fulfillment.

What makes Mary's role even more poignant is the sacrificial dimension intertwined with her assent. Her yes was not merely a one-time affirmation; it was a lifelong embrace of God's will, culminating in the sorrowful yet redemptive co-suffering with her son. At the foot of the Cross, Mary's heart pierced by the sword of sorrow as foretold by Simeon, she stands as a testament to unwavering faith and fiat. As the New Eve, her cooperation with God's redemptive plan highlights her pivotal role in salvation history.

The typology of Mary as the New Eve also provides profound insights for the spiritual journey of the Knights of Columbus. The knightly mission, imbued with vows of charity, unity, and fraternity, finds a Marian model in its quest for virtue and holiness. Just as Mary's obedience and humility brought forth redemption, so too can the knights' devotion and commitment bring forth the grace of God in their lives and communities.

This understanding imbues Marian consecration with sacramental depth. Through devotion to Mary, they not only honor the mother of God but participate in the divine mystery of salvation through their own acts of faith and obedience. The symbolism of Mary as the New Eve can serve as a constant reminder of their call to embody virtues of fidelity, courage, and love, mirroring the unwavering faith of Mary.

Furthermore, the image of Mary as the New Eve carries rich liturgical significance. In prayers, hymns, and feasts dedicated to her, the Church invites the faithful to reflect upon this typological connection. Think of the joyous celebrations of the Annunciation, the Immaculate Conception, and the Solemnity of Mary, Mother of God. Each serves as a liturgical tapestry, weaving together the narrative of salvation history, with Mary at its heart as the New Eve.

The allegorical imagery of Mary as the New Eve also finds resonance in the visual arts. Icons and paintings often depict Mary with symbols that allude to her role in the new creation. The contrast between the old Eve often shown with the apple, a symbol of fallen humanity, and Mary depicted with Christ or the lily of purity, encapsulates this transformative typology.

In conclusion, the Blessed Virgin Mary as the New Eve enriches our understanding of the Incarnation and the redemptive mission of Jesus Christ. It is a narrative thread that binds the Old and New Testaments, offering a panoramic view of God's salvation plan. For the Knights of Columbus, this typology is more than a theological concept; it is a call to live out their Marian devotion in a manner that transforms their hearts and communities, elevating their service to a participation in the divine mystery.

Mary as the Ark of the Covenant

In the vast and luminous tapestry of divine revelation, Mary stands out as a figure prefigured by various archetypes in the Old Testament. One of the most profound typologies is that of Mary as the Ark of the Covenant. Just as the Ark of the Covenant was the sacred vessel containing the presence of God, so too is Mary the living Ark who bore within her womb Jesus Christ, the Word made flesh.

Let's turn our gaze to the ancient Ark that accompanied the Israelites. Constructed by the skilled craftsmanship of Bezalel, under the command of Moses, according to God's design, the Ark was crafted from acacia wood and overlaid with pure gold. In it were placed the stone tablets of the Ten Commandments, a jar of manna, and Aaron's rod that had budded. These were the symbols of God's covenant, providence, and priesthood. The Ark was so holy that to touch it improperly meant death, as evidenced by the fate of Uzzah. It was a beacon of God's presence among His people, residing in the Holy of Holies, behind the veil in the tabernacle and later in the temple.

The Ark's importance to the Israelites cannot be overstated. It led them through the wilderness, crossed over the Jordan, and brought down the walls of Jericho. It was at the very center of their worship and their understanding of God's immanence. Now, consider Mary, whose very being was prepared by God to be a pure and untouched vessel. The interplay between these two arks unfolds a narrative of divine orchestration and loving foresight.

In the Gospel of Luke, the angel Gabriel announces to Mary, "The Holy Spirit will come upon you, and the power of the Most High will overshadow you; therefore, the child to be born will be called holy—the Son of God" (Luke 1:35). The word "overshadow" used here is also found in the Septuagint in describing how the Shekinah glory cloud overshadowed the Ark. This divine overshadowing signifies God's presence. Such a parallel infuses the Annunciation with significance, portraying Mary as the Ark within whom the divine Logos chose to dwell.

Furthermore, we see Mary as the Ark in her visitation to Elizabeth. When Mary enters Elizabeth's home, John the Baptist leaps in Elizabeth's womb. Elizabeth, filled with the Holy Spirit, exclaims, "And why is this granted to me that the mother of my Lord should come to me?" (Luke 1:43). This mirrors King David's reaction when the Ark was brought to Jerusalem: "How can the ark of the Lord come to me?" (2 Samuel 6:9). The joy expressed by Elizabeth and the unborn John parallels David's leaping before the Ark, further reinforcing Mary as the Ark bearing God's presence.

In another sense, Mary's Ark carried the New Covenant—a covenant written not on stone tablets but inscribed upon human hearts by the Holy Spirit. It is through Mary's "fiat," her willing consent to God's plan, that the Word took on flesh and inaugurated the new covenant. The bread from heaven in the old Ark prefigures the true Bread of Life, Jesus Christ, whom Mary carried. Aaron's rod that budded, symbolizing God's chosen priesthood, prefigures Jesus, the eternal High Priest.

The image of Mary as the Ark also illuminates her role within the community of the faithful. Just as the Ark went ahead of the Israelites, guiding them and ensuring their victory, Mary precedes the Church in her perfect discipleship. Her Assumption into heaven, body and soul, is seen as a sign of the eschatological promise to which the Church aspires. Mary, the Ark, now resides in the heavenly Holy of Holies, advocating and interceding for us.

For the Knights of Columbus, devoted to Marian consecration, understanding Mary as the Ark of the Covenant deepens the appreciation of her singular role in salvation history. As Knights commit themselves to Mary, they are aligning with the divine order Moses, David, and the prophets followed—reverencing the holy vessel which bore God's presence. This metaphor further establishes that Marian devotion is not peripheral but central to the Christian life.

In consecrating themselves to Mary, Knights are, in a way, choosing to follow the Ark. They acknowledge her as the custodian of the divine mysteries who always points to her Son, Jesus. This journey is one of spiritual combat and pilgrimage, reminiscent of the Israelites' wanderings with the Ark. Mary, our Ark, guides us safely through the treacherous terrain of earthly life, helping us to overcome the Jerichos we encounter.

The depth of this typology invites further contemplation and devotion. Mary as the Ark signifies purity, God's presence, and divine guidance. Her "yes" to God resounds through the ages, inviting us to enter into this divine mystery more fully. For as the Ark was at the heart of Israel's worship and devotion, so should Mary be central to our consecration, leading us to the heart of the Holy Trinity.

As the story of our salvation unfolds, Mary stands as a testament to God's intricate plan. Embracing her as the Ark is not merely an act of reverence but a profound participation in God's divine will. Like the Israelites of old, we follow her, bearing the promise of God's covenant in our hearts.

Mary as the Ark of the Covenant encapsulates her unique role, offering us a touchstone for deeper faith and a richer understanding of the mysteries we hold dear.

Mary as the Queen of Heaven

In contemplating the regal title of Mary as the Queen of Heaven, we ascend into an ethereal domain of profound meaning and grace. This epithet isn't just figurative; it carries deep theological implications that form a tapestry of Marian devotion. The Mother of God, crowned in celestial splendor, stands as a beacon of unwavering faith and intercessory power, a true queen who assumes her position with humility and love.

The roots of this majestic title are anchored in Sacred Scripture and breathed to life through the Church's tradition. In the Old Testament, we find prefigurements that hint at Mary's queenship. For instance, in Psalm 45, the psalmist speaks of a queen standing at the king's right hand, adorned in gold from Ophir. This imagery of royal dignity and grandeur culminates in the New Testament through the revelation of Mary's ultimate role and status. The Book of Revelation offers a majestic vision where "a great sign appeared in heaven: a woman clothed with the sun, with the moon under her feet and a crown of twelve stars on her head" (Revelation 12:1).

This celestial vision not only evokes wonder but also aligns Mary with a regal authority granted by divine providence. Her queenship is intrinsically linked to her motherhood of Jesus, the King of Kings. Just as Solomon's mother Bathsheba sat at his right hand (1 Kings 2:19), Mary is enthroned alongside her Son, reflecting a role filled with divine purpose.

St. Louis de Montfort eloquently speaks of Mary as the Queen of all hearts, emphasizing her maternal reign over the souls committed to Christ. In this light, her queenship is far from an earthly dominion; it's a compassionate rule that seeks to bring every soul closer to her Son. Her crown symbolizes victory and triumph, not over nations of this world, but over the forces of sin and death.

Moreover, Mary's queenship extends into her intercessory role. Her seat in heaven is not one of passive rest but active involvement. Like the Queen Mother in ancient Israel who acted as an advocate for the people, Mary intercedes for us with an unparalleled efficacy. The depth of her intercession is such that it bends the ear of God, a true testimony to the boundless love she bears for humanity. Her advocacy is a direct fruit of her intimate union with the Holy Trinity, making her an ever-available channel of divine grace.

One might reflect on Mary's queenship by drawing parallels to her distinctive titles and roles delineated throughout the Bible. She is the New Eve, who through her obedience and faith becomes the Mother of all the living in the realm of grace. As the Ark of the Covenant, she bears within her the presence of God in Jesus Christ, making her a sacred vessel of divine life and promise. Each of these titles collectively underscores her sovereign role as Queen of Heaven.

The Venerable Archbishop Fulton Sheen beautifully affirms, "Jesus is King of Heaven and Earth; in his kingdom, he has reserved a most exalted place for his Blessed Mother." Such reflections reinforce the privilege and honor bestowed upon Mary, not merely as acts of veneration but as acknowledgment of her unique participatory role in the economy of salvation.

In the prayers and liturgies of the Roman Catholic Church, Mary's queenship is universally acknowledged. The "Hail, Holy Queen" prayer encapsulates our longing and trust in her intercessory power: "Hail, Holy Queen, Mother of Mercy, our life, our sweetness, and our hope." These are not just words recited in devotion but a proclamation of her protective and nurturing kingship. The liturgical feast of the Queenship of Mary further emphasizes this recognition, celebrated on August 22, following the Solemnity of the Assumption. Both feasts are intimately connected, portraying Mary's entry into heavenly glory and royal exaltation.

Indeed, through the lens of Marian devotion, we view Mary's queenship as an enduring mystery and a beckoning call. For the Knights of Columbus, it becomes a paradigm of service and devotion. The Knights, known for their unwavering commitment to the Church and Marian devotion, find in Mary a model of humility wrapped in glory, service shrouded in honor, and love epitomized by her queenship. Their knighthood reflects the celestial knighthood where serving the Queen means serving Christ.

The allegorical dimension of Mary as Queen is rich with layers of spiritual meaning. Each nuance of her title invites us deeper, from the Marian hymns that serenade her as Queen of Angels to the scriptural references that decorate her with an aura of divine majesty. We see her through the prophetic eyes of Isaiah, adorned in beauty and splendor. Through the symbolic language of Revelation, she stands victorious, her queenship celebrated by the celestial hosts.

As we delve into doctrinal formulations, the Dogma of the Assumption indirectly underscores her queenship. Pius XII's "Munificentissimus Deus" highlights how Mary was assumed body and soul into heavenly glory. The logical and theological consequence follows: if she is in heavenly glory, she participates in the royal dignity of her Son. Her queenship is thus not an honorary title but one imbued with the fullness of heavenly life, deeply rooted in her role in the Divine Plan.

Her queenship is also a call to each Knight to imitate her virtues. Courage, humility, and unwavering faith are the jewels in her crown—jewels that every Knight should aspire to possess. Serving under the mantle of the Queen of Heaven means embracing these virtues as guiding principles in one's life. The Knights of Columbus, in their mission to uphold the Church's teachings and serve the community, find in Mary the quintessential model of loyal service and maternal care.

In conclusion, Mary as the Queen of Heaven is more than a title—it's an invitation. An invitation to reflect on the profound relationship between Mother and Son, between Queen and her subjects, and between the divine and the human. For the Knights of Columbus, this title embodies a spiritual ethos that calls for a life of service, devotion, and active participation in the mission of the Church. As we recognize Mary's queenship, we accept the call to deeper consecration and commitment, journeying towards the ultimate union with the Holy Trinity through the loving intercession of our Queen.

Mary prefigured by Sarah, Queen Esther, the Maccabees Mother, the Ark of the Covenant, Judith, and Jael

The mystical connections between the Blessed Virgin Mary and key figures in the Old Testament are profound and vivid, echoing the timeless themes of faith, courage, and divine providence. In this section, we explore how Mary is prefigured by Sarah, Queen Esther, the Maccabees Mother, the Ark of the Covenant, Judith, and Jael. These scriptural typologies provide rich allegories, underscoring Mary's role as a pivotal figure in salvation history.

Sarah, the wife of Abraham, stands as an early reflection of Mary. Like Mary, Sarah was promised a miraculous birth, illustrating divine intervention in human history. Just as Sarah bore Isaac in her old age, fulfilling God's promise, Mary bore Jesus through the Holy Spirit, confirming God's eternal covenant with His chosen people. Sarah's joyful laughter echoes Mary's Magnificat, a song of praise to God for His wondrous deeds.

Moving from the matriarchal to the royal, Queen Esther offers another compelling parallel. Esther's story is one of bravery and divine favor. Chosen to be queen, she risked her life to save her people from destruction. Her intercession with King Ahasuerus foreshadows Mary's intercession for humanity with Jesus. Just as Esther achieved deliverance for her people, Mary, through her 'yes', brings forth the Savior, securing our spiritual deliverance.

Another poignant figure is the Maccabees Mother. According to Second Maccabees, this mother exhibits profound faith and courage as she watches her seven sons endure martyrdom rather than break God's law. Her steadfast faith underlines the strength of maternal devotion, paralleled in Mary's unwavering faith at the foot of the Cross. Both she and Mary experienced the pinnacle of maternal suffering, yet their faith remained unshaken, serving as potent symbols of persevering belief in divine will.

The Ark of the Covenant is perhaps one of the most enigmatic yet profound prefigurations of Mary. The Ark, a sacred chest built to carry the most holy objects of Israel, including the tablets of the Law, the manna, and Aaron's rod, symbolizes God's presence among His people. Likewise, Mary is the new Ark, bearing within her womb Jesus Christ, the Word made Flesh. The Ark carried God's covenant; Mary brought forth the New Covenant through her son. This typology reinforces the notion that Mary's purity and her role as the bearer of divine grace are intrinsic to Christian faith.

Judith, another courageous woman from the Old Testament, also prefigures Mary. Judith's victory over Holofernes, an enemy general, through her bravery and reliance on God, mirrors Mary's spiritual victory. Just as Judith's triumph brought liberation to her people, Mary's acceptance to bear the Son of God heralded a new era of redemption and grace. Both women's stories highlight divine strength manifesting through apparent vulnerability.

Lastly, Jael, known for her decisive action in the book of Judges, offers a striking symbol of deliverance. By defeating the oppressive Sisera with a single blow, Jael plays a critical role in securing Israel's victory. This act of unexpected heroism prefigures Mary's role in the ultimate victory over sin and death. Through her humble acceptance and faithfulness, Mary crushes the serpent's head as foretold in Genesis, symbolizing the defeat of evil.

These biblical figures not only illuminate Mary's unique role in God's salvific plan but also inspire devotion among the faithful. Each story, rich in symbolism and meaning, beckons us to delve deeper into the mystery of Mary's divine mission. The Blessed Mother, as prefigured by Sarah, Queen Esther, the Maccabees Mother, the Ark of the Covenant, Judith, and Jael, stands as an eternal testament to God's unwavering love and providence.

True to the tradition of the Knights of Columbus, these typological connections call us to a deeper consecration, encouraging us to embrace the virtues of faith, courage, and trust in divine will. By understanding these profound prefigurations, our devotion to Mary intensifies, allowing us to draw closer to the Trinity through her. The allegories of these Old Testament figures weave a rich tapestry that not only enhances our spiritual understanding but also enriches our journey as devoted Catholics.

Thus, as we contemplate these scriptural connections, let them not be mere historical reflections, but living, breathing inspirations that guide our actions and deepen our commitment to our consecration. In recognizing Mary prefigured by these heroic and faithful women, we reaffirm our dedication to living out our faith with the same fervor and devotion. This is the profound legacy left for us to treasure and emulate, mirroring the eternal truths revealed through Mary and all who prefigured her significant role in salvation history.

Chapter 5: Developing a Heart for Consecration

In the realm of knights and devotees, developing a heart for consecration is like embarking on a sacred quest. It's a transformative journey where every prayer, practice, and act of devotion illuminates the path toward a deeper union with the Trinity through Mary, our celestial guide. With each Rosary bead slid through our fingers, and every Hail Mary spoken from our lips, we cultivate a life centered around unwavering devotion. This consecration isn't mere ritual; it's the lifeblood of our spiritual knighthood. We learn to offer our daily trials and triumphs to the Lord through the immaculate heart of Mary, who, like a mother cradling her cherished child, tenderly brings our intentions before the Holy Trinity. It is through this consecrated heart that we discover the profound mystery and joy of our faith, standing as beacons of divine light in a world yearning for God's love.

Cultivating a Devotional Life

Embarking on the journey to develop a heart for consecration begins with cultivating a devotional life that bridges our daily existence with the divine. This path, much like a winding forest trail lit by dappled sunlight, guides Knights of Columbus into deeper communion with the Holy Trinity through the tender advocacy of the Blessed Mother. It is in the quiet, consistent rhythms of devotion where our spiritual armor is fortified, and our hearts are shaped in the mold of divine love.

In the rich tapestry of Roman Catholic tradition, daily acts of devotion serve as threads that weave us closer to the sacred heart of Christ. These acts, varying in simplicity and grandeur, draw us into that mystical union where our earthly lives touch the hem of eternity. Devotional life isn't inherently complex; rather, it is formed from consistent, heartfelt practices that align us with heavenly virtues.

The morning offers a pure canvas, an opportunity to consecrate the day's first moments to God. Picture the early riser, greeting the dawn with a whispered prayer or a hymn dedicated to the Blessed Mother. These initial steps set the tone for the hours that follow, casting a sanctified glow on all endeavors. Just as King David declared, "O Lord, in the morning you hear my voice; in the morning I prepare a sacrifice for you and watch" (Psalm 5:3), so too do we offer our fresh beginnings as a sacred tribute.

Yet, cultivating a devotional life is not confined to morning rituals alone. The Rosary, a revered cornerstone of Marian devotion, is a powerful, meditative prayer that can be integrated into various parts of the day. Each bead we finger, each mystery we contemplate, draws us closer to understanding our Savior through the heart of our Blessed Mother. This prayerful rhythm chimes with the heartbeat of our faith, providing not just solace but profound spiritual insight.

Consider the midday Angelus, a tradition that halts the daily grind to recall the Incarnation's mystery. At noon, imagine the workman's tools laid down, the clamor of industry pausing, as faithful hands clasp in silent reverence. Enshrining such moments in our routine fortifies our resolve and wraps our mundane activities in divine purpose. It transports our spirits to that sacred intersection where heaven touches earth.

As the day's light wanes, the Liturgy of the Hours invites us to pause and pray once more, synchronizing our lives with the Church's universal prayer. Evening prayers soothe the weary soul, offering rest in the companionship of saints and angels. The Examen of St. Ignatius, a reflective practice, allows us to review our day, acknowledge divine encounters, and seek forgiveness for our shortcomings. This sacred scrutiny masks nothing, for it is a mirror held by the loving hand of God.

A strong devotional life also blossoms through the Sacraments, lifelines of grace that sustain and rejuvenate our spiritual journey. Regular confession purifies and enriches the soul, mending the cracks born of sin and restoring us to holiness. The Eucharist is the summit of our devotion, with Christ's real presence feeding our deepest hunger and quenching our profoundest thirst. In this divine feast, our consecration is both remembered and renewed.

Beyond individual practices, communal devotion strengthens our bonds with each other and amplifies our collective faith. Knights of Columbus, bound together by principles of charity, unity, and fraternity, find in shared acts of devotion a powerful testament to God's love in action. Group Rosaries, prayer meetings, and pilgrimages become a tapestry of fervent faith, each thread weaving a story of divine grace experienced in community.

Indeed, the Marian consecration renewals, often conducted as a collective ritual, signify a profound shared commitment to our Blessed Mother as our spiritual guide and intercessor. Held on significant feast days or as part of a novena, these renewals echo with the vows of countless knights who have walked this path before us, creating a spiritual symphony that transcends time.

In the quiet folds of our day-to-day lives, sacramentals serve as blessed companions, relics of our devotion that draw us nearer to God. A Miraculous Medal worn around the neck, a scapular resting over the heart, or holy water sprinkled within our homes; these sacred items are not mere symbols but conduits of grace. They are reminders of our continual consecration to the Trinity through Mary, enveloping us in a tangible cloak of divine protection and love.

Stories and lives of the saints also play a pivotal role in nurturing our devotional practices. Their lives, mirrored in our own, offer a roadmap of holiness and perseverance. St. Maximilian Kolbe's relentless dedication, showcasing Marian devotion even in the direst conditions, paints a vivid picture of ultimate surrender. St. Louis de Montfort's deep theological insights on Marian consecration provide a rich resource to deepen our understanding and commitment. Emulating such saints fuels our zeal and fortifies our own spiritual resolve.

The beauty of cultivating a devotional life lies in its accessibility to all. It doesn't demand grand gestures or erudition but rather an open heart and a willing spirit. It invites us to see the divine in the ordinary, to transform every moment into a prayer, and to live with constant awareness of God's presence in our midst. This journey of devotion, wrapped in the mantle of our Blessed Mother, leads us unfailingly to the heart of the Trinity.

Aligned with the daily rhythms of prayer, sacraments, and communal acts of faith, our lives are sanctified, steeped in grace and divine love. Even as we navigate the challenges and trials of our earthly pilgrimage, these devotional practices anchor us, ensuring that our hearts remain consecrated at every beat, whispering unwaveringly our commitment to God through Mary.

Daily Practices for Devotion

In the journey of developing a heart for consecration, daily practices play a crucial role. These practices serve as the humble offerings to Our Blessed Mother and, through her, to the Most Holy Trinity. They are the lifeblood of one's spiritual commitment, a steady stream that nourishes and sustains fervor. Each day presents an opportunity to renew and deepen our consecration, helping us to live out our devotion in tangible and meaningful ways.

First, begin each day with a sincere Morning Offering. Upon waking, even before your feet touch the ground, offer your day to God through Mary. This simple act of consecration sanctifies the day ahead, dedicating all your thoughts, words, and actions to the service of the Holy Trinity. This practice echoes the fiat of Mary, her "yes" to God's will, and sets the tone for a life lived in constant offer to the divine plan.

Next, incorporate the Rosary into your daily routine. The Rosary is not merely a collection of prayers but a powerful meditation on the lives of Jesus and Mary. Each bead, each mystery, draws you closer to the heart of the Gospel, and through this rhythm, you enter into a deep communion with the divine. Whether prayed in silent contemplation at dawn or as a family in the evening, this devotion is a fortress against the distractions and temptations of the world.

Varying the mysteries based on the day of the week—Joyful, Sorrowful, Glorious, and Luminous—root us in the different aspects of Christ's life and mission. Each mystery is a window into the sacred, allowing divine grace to pour into our daily lives. Remember to pray not only for your intentions but also for the intentions of those around you, creating a web of intercession that binds the community in love and support.

In addition to the Rosary, make time for the Divine Office or the Liturgy of the Hours. This ancient practice, rooted in the Psalms, sanctifies the entire day at regular intervals—morning, midday, evening, and night. Joining your voice with the universal Church, you're reminded that your devotion is part of a grand tapestry of prayer, lifting the whole world to God. For the busy Knight, even praying a selected hour, such as Lauds in the morning or Vespers in the evening, can be incredibly enriching.

Engaging with Sacred Scripture daily is another pillar of a devotional life. The Bible is the living word of God, and through it, He speaks personally to each one of us. Allow a few moments each day for Lectio Divina, a meditative reading of the Scriptures where you can listen deeply and respond in your heart. Contemplating the life of Mary as she appears in the Gospels enriches our understanding of her role in salvation history and our devotion to her.

In your daily actions, strive to practice virtues, particularly those exemplified by Mary. Humility, obedience, purity, and charity are more than just ideals—they are pathways to living a consecrated life. Seek opportunities to serve others, especially in your local community. Small acts of kindness and service, performed in the spirit of Mary, reflect the love of Christ and promote a culture of fraternity and holiness.

A powerful yet often overlooked practice is the Angelus. Traditionally prayed at 6 a.m., 12 p.m., and 6 p.m., this brief devotion recalls the Incarnation, the moment the Word became flesh. It punctuates the day with reminders of God's ineffable love and Mary's pivotal role in His plan. Interrupting the busyness of daily tasks, the Angelus brings a moment of peace and reflection, redirecting our hearts to the divine mysteries.

Eucharistic Adoration provides a profound encounter with Jesus in the Blessed Sacrament. Spending time before the Eucharist, whether in silent adoration, prayer, or simply resting in His presence, deepens our relationship with Christ and anchors our devotion. The Knights of Columbus often organize eucharistic adoration events, offering a communal dimension to this sacred practice. During these times, present your sorrows, joys, and intentions to the Lord, and listen for His guidance.

Regular participation in the Sacrament of Reconciliation is vital. This sacrament of mercy cleanses the soul, providing the grace needed to overcome sin and grow in holiness. Through confession, we are spiritually renewed and fortified, better equipped to live our consecration. Approach this sacrament not as a mechanical obligation, but as a heartfelt encounter with God's boundless mercy.

Lastly, embody the Marian virtues in your personal apostolate. Let your light shine before others, reflecting Mary's humility, purity, and unwavering faith in your interactions. Whether it's through teaching catechism, supporting parish activities, or simply being a compassionate presence, your actions can speak volumes about the transformative power of Marian consecration.

As you integrate these daily practices into your life, remember that true devotion is not about the quantity of prayers, but the quality of your love and commitment. It is a dynamic relationship, ever deepening and expanding as you grow closer to Jesus through Mary. Each day becomes a step on the pilgrimage of faith, leading you to a fuller union with the Holy Trinity. In this sacred journey, you'll find that your heart, much like Mary's, becomes a vessel of divine grace, bringing light and love to a world in need.

Chapter 6: The Commandments and Living the Divine Will

When we engage with the Commandments, we are not merely adhering to a set of rules dictated by an external authority; we are embracing a path that leads us closer to the heart of God's Divine

Will. This sacred journey requires our whole being, urging us to elevate our actions, thoughts, and desires toward Heaven. Living the Divine Will means syncing our innermost essence with the beatitudes of the Ten Commandments, transforming obedience from a duty to a delight. It's through this harmonious alignment that we Knights of Columbus and devoted children of the Blessed Mother become true instruments of His grace. As we integrate these divine precepts into our daily lives, we manifest the Kingdom of God on Earth, echoing the ancient wisdom of the prophets and the timeless love of Christ. Our consecration is fortified as we live out these commandments, embodying a profound testament to the faith we hold dear and the divine mission we are called to fulfill.

Embracing the Ten Commandments

The Ten Commandments, given to Moses on Mount Sinai, are not just a set of rules; they are keys to living in harmony with the divine will. For the Knights of Columbus, these commandments are a guiding light, illuminating the path to a deeper, more committed consecration to the Holy Trinity through Mother Mary. Each commandment represents a facet of divine love and wisdom, calling us to align our lives with God's eternal plan.

Embracing the Ten Commandments starts with understanding their significance. The first three commandments are about our relationship with God: to recognize Him as the one true God, to honor His name, and to keep the Sabbath holy. These commandments anchor us in worship and reverence, urging us to place God at the center of our lives. In doing so, we acknowledge that our strength and purpose derive from Him. Devotion to Mother Mary helps us to fulfill these commandments more perfectly, as she always leads us to her Son.

The fourth commandment, "Honor your father and mother," broadens our understanding of respect and obedience. For Knights of Columbus, this commandment extends to honoring the Church as our mother and respecting our spiritual fathers—our priests and bishops. By upholding and supporting the hierarchy of the Church, we ensure the continuity and integrity of our faith. This commandment invites us to foster familial bonds, promoting love and unity within our families and communities.

Commandments five through ten focus on our relationships with others. They teach us to respect life, practice fidelity, recognize others' dignity and property, speak truthfully, and avoid coveting. These commandments form the moral bedrock of social justice and personal integrity. They are not mere prohibitions but invitations to live virtuously. Living by these commandments transforms our interactions, making us beacons of God's love and justice.

Embracing the Ten Commandments is not about strict legalism but about entering into a covenant of love with God and neighbor. As Knights, we are called to be exemplary in our conduct, mirroring Christ's love and compassion. Each commandment calls us to a deeper conversion of heart, urging us to go beyond mere compliance to a heartfelt commitment to God's will. In this journey, Mother Mary stands as our model and intercessor, embodying perfect obedience and love.

Practical application of the Ten Commandments within our daily lives can be challenging but deeply rewarding. It involves constant vigilance and discernment, ensuring our actions reflect our faith. This commitment to living the commandments should permeate every aspect of our lives—our work, family, community engagements, and private prayers. In doing so, we become living testimonies of God's grace and mercy.

Moreover, the Ten Commandments serve as a framework for introspection and confession. Regular examination of conscience allows us to identify where we've faltered and seek reconciliation through the sacrament of penance. This practice not only purifies us but also strengthens our resolve to live more faithfully. By frequently turning to Mother Mary, we can find the strength and grace needed to adhere to God's commandments with joy and dedication.

Living the Ten Commandments also fosters a spirit of unity. As Knights, our actions influence many, and adhering to these divine precepts unites us in a common mission. It creates a harmonious environment where mutual respect and love flourish. In our councils, parishes, and neighborhoods, we become instruments of peace, witnessing to the transformative power of divine law.

The Ten Commandments are timeless truths, relevant in every age and culture. They provide a blueprint for a holy life that is pleasing to God. By embracing these commandments wholeheartedly, we align ourselves with divine wisdom and open our hearts to the transformative power of grace. We become not only guardians of the faith but also its radiant exemplars.

As Knights of Columbus devoted to Marian Consecration, living according to the Ten Commandments is a profound expression of our consecration. It is through obedience to God's law and a sincere devotion to Mary that we can draw closer to the Holy Trinity. Our consecration gains depth and authenticity as we strive to live out these sacred commandments daily, allowing their principles to shape our hearts and guide our steps.

In conclusion, embracing the Ten Commandments is an indispensable part of living the divine will. It's a journey that requires effort, sacrifice, and, most importantly, grace. Mother Mary, who perfectly lived these commandments, is our guide and advocate in this endeavor. By faithfully following these divine laws, we grow in holiness and become true knights of Christ and His Blessed Mother, prepared to advance the cause of the Kingdom of God in our world. Let's embrace these commandments with unwavering commitment, knowing that in doing so, we walk the path that leads to eternal life with God.

Living According to the Divine Will

To live according to the Divine Will is to align one's very existence with the perfect plan of God. This alignment isn't conceived merely in grand gestures but in every thought, action, and intention. By embracing the Ten Commandments, we establish the foundational principles upon which this divine architecture stands. Each commandment acts as a boundary and a beacon, guiding us through the moral landscapes of our daily lives.

Our Blessed Mother, the pinnacle of human obedience to God, provides the ultimate blueprint. Her complete submission to God's will was not marked by extraordinary moments alone, but through her "fiat" – a simple yet profound acceptance of God's plan. By contemplating her life, we can understand that living according to the Divine Will requires humility, patience, and an unshakeable trust in God's providence.

The Knights of Columbus, consecrated to the Trinity through Mary, are called to a heightened awareness and commitment to this path. Living according to the Divine Will means more than ful-filling rites or practicing pious devotions. It demands a deep internal transformation, where every aspect of our being resonates with divine harmony. This is accomplished through a constant conver-sion of heart and mind, rooted in prayer and sustained by the sacraments.

One might ask, what does this look like in practical terms? It begins with an earnest examination of conscience. Often, we find that our desires, though well-intentioned, can diverge from God's will. By regularly reflecting on our actions and intentions, we identify and prune those desires that lead us away from divine alignment. The sacrament of reconciliation becomes a vital tool in this spiritual gardening, offering grace to correct our course.

Living out the Divine Will also means living the beatitudes. These teachings of Christ outline the virtues that flourish when we trust and submit to God's plan. Blessed are the poor in spirit, those who mourn, the meek, and the merciful – each beatitude represents a facet of living according to the Divine Will. They teach us to embrace our weaknesses and offer them to God, allowing His strength to work through us.

Consider the virtue of meekness, often misunderstood as weakness. In the light of divine will, meekness represents a gentle strength, a quiet resilience that submits all to God without complaint or resistance. It's the strength Our Lady showed at the foot of the Cross, a profound acceptance of suffering united with a steadfast trust in divine providence.

For the Knights of Columbus, this path isn't walked alone. The fraternal support among the brothers provides encouragement and accountability. Together, we encourage one another to keep our eyes fixed on Christ and our hearts attuned to His will. In our communal prayers, meetings, and acts of service, we find the strength to live out this profound calling.

The family too, becomes a crucial battleground for living the Divine Will. In our roles as fathers, sons, husbands, and brothers, we encounter numerous opportunities for self-giving love and humil-ity. Our homes should reflect this sacred commitment, becoming sanctuaries where God's presence is felt, and His will is paramount. Simple acts of kindness, forgiveness, and shared prayer can trans-form our families into vibrant cells of God's Kingdom.

It is also essential to recognize that this alignment with the Divine Will is an ongoing journey. We must continuously seek God's guidance through prayer, scripture, and the teachings of the Church. The writings of the saints, particularly those devoted to Marian spirituality, offer rich insights into living according to the Divine Will. They illuminate pathways we might have missed, helping us to navigate the complexities of modern life while remaining rooted in divine truth.

Moreover, our engagement with the world provides yet another canvas on which to paint our fidelity to God's will. In our professions, social interactions, and civic duties, we are called to be Christ's ambassadors. Every decision we make, every word we speak, should reflect our consecration to the Divine Will. This might mean standing up for truth in the face of opposition or offering com-passion in situations marred by indifference.

The Eucharist stands at the center of our efforts to live the Divine Will. In this sacrament, Jesus offers His very body and blood, uniting us intimately with His sacrifice. Every Mass becomes an in-vitation to deeper conformity with Him, drawing us into His perfect obedience to the Father. Our participation in the Eucharist should inspire us to offer our lives more fully to God's plan, echoing Christ's words, "Not my will, but Yours be done."

Living according to the Divine Will also involves a certain detachment from worldly goods and ambitions. While we partake in the world's activities, we remain anchored in heaven's values. This detachment doesn't manifest as neglect of our responsibilities but as a freedom to pursue God's purposes without being ensnared by material concerns. It calls for wise stewardship, using our resources to further God's Kingdom rather than seeking our own gain.

In this journey, patience becomes a cherished ally. God's timing often diverges from our own, and His paths may lead us through valleys before we reach mountaintops. Emulating Mary's patient trust, we wait upon the Lord, confident that His plans are for our ultimate good. The trials we endure, the sacrifices we make, all become copper threads in the tapestry God weaves from our lives.

Every Knight of Columbus is tasked with embodying this divine orientation in the broader society. It manifests in ethical business practices, integrity in politics, and compassion in community service. By living according to the Divine Will, we become lights in a world often shrouded in darkness, pointing others towards the ultimate source of truth and love.

As we strive to live according to the Divine Will, let us continually invoke the guidance of the Blessed Virgin Mary. Her maternal intercession and exemplary life are invaluable aids on this path. Through her, we better understand what it means to surrender completely to God and to live in the joy and freedom of His divine love.

Chapter 7: The Virtues and Natural Law

The harmonious orchestration of virtues and natural law serves as the keystone in our journey to consecrate ourselves to the Holy Trinity through Mary. Cardinal virtues—prudence, justice, fortitude, and temperance—are not merely classical ideals but living guides etched in the law of our hearts by the Creator's hand. As Knights of Columbus, imbued with Marian devotion, we transform these virtues into acts of love and charity, bearing witness to the eternal truths of natural law. This divine wisdom, as solid as the rock of Peter, calls us to act justly, love sincerely, and walk humbly with our God. In aligning our lives with these principles, we engage in a sacred dance, echoing the rhythm of the universe's original design and reflecting the seamless unity between divine will and human freedom.

Understanding Cardinal Virtues

The Cardinal Virtues are the cornerstones of moral life, guiding us toward a righteous path illuminated by faith and reason. In Roman Catholic theology, they serve as the essential bedrock upon which all other virtues rest. Born of practical wisdom and ancient traditions, these virtues are Prudence, Justice, Fortitude, and Temperance. Each one, distinct in its scope, contributes to a harmonious life attuned to God's will.

Let's begin with Prudence, often dubbed the "charioteer of virtues." It isn't merely cautiousness; it is the golden thread that guides our moral compass. Prudence involves discernment—choosing the right means to achieve good ends. In the words of St. Thomas Aquinas, it's "right reason in action." This virtue calls for a thoughtful pause before action, weaving the wisdom of the past with the keen awareness of the present, preparing us for future challenges. In the complexity of life's moral dilemmas, Prudence provides clarity, allowing us to navigate with foresight and sagacity.

Next, we have Justice. This virtue is more than rendering each their due. It embodies a profound commitment to fairness, equity, and the common good. Justice, in its purest form, mirrors divine order, where all creation is harmoniously balanced. It challenges us to uphold the dignity of every individual, from the unborn to the elderly, and to engage actively in societal structures that reflect God's own righteous order. Whether in interpersonal relationships or broader societal contexts, Justice is an unwavering beacon, urging us to act justly, love mercy, and walk humbly with our God.

Fortitude, or courage, is the virtue that emboldens us to stand firm in the face of adversity. It's the strength to overcome obstacles and to persist in doing good despite fear and opposition. Fortitude is not reckless bravery but a valor grounded in conviction and rooted in faith. It lends us the resilience to bear suffering and the perseverance to pursue virtue even when the path is steep and rocky. Through Fortitude, we find the divine courage to carry our crosses, mirroring the steadfastness of saints and martyrs who have walked before us.

Finally, Temperance brings balance and self-control into our lives. It regulates our appetites and desires, ensuring that they serve our higher purpose rather than enslaving us. Temperance is the harmonious orchestra of the soul, where each desire plays in tune with God's design. It fosters moderation in all things, allowing us to enjoy life's pleasures in a way that uplifts rather than diminishes our dignity. By practicing Temperance, we embrace a life of simplicity and humility, keeping us attuned to the divine rhythm.

These four virtues form an interlocking framework, each enhancing and supporting the others. Prudence without Justice can lead to cunning; Justice without Fortitude can become passive; Fortitude without Temperance can devolve into recklessness; and Temperance without Prudence can turn into asceticism. Thus, to embody one fully is to be rooted in them all, creating a well-rounded character that reflects divine image.

As Knights of Columbus, these Cardinal Virtues serve not merely as ideals but as pragmatic guides in our daily lives. They shape our interactions, decisions, and ultimately, our journey toward sanctification. These virtues mold us into men who are not just pious but just, not just cautious but wise, not just brave but faithful, and not just moderate but free.

Furthermore, these virtues align harmoniously with the Natural Law, the moral code inherent in human nature. Natural Law, inscribed by God in the heart of every person, showcases the blueprint for achieving human flourishing. It underscores that moral truths are not arbitrary but rooted in the divine order, comprehensible through reason and revealed through faith. The Cardinal Virtues are the practical expressions of these eternal truths, encapsulating how we can live according to Natural Law.

Living out these virtues doesn't require heroic feats but faithfulness in small, everyday actions. It means being prudent in our decisions, just in our dealings, courageous in our struggles, and temperate in our desires. It involves seeing every mundane task and every fleeting moment as an opportunity to practice virtue, thereby sanctifying the temporal and integrating the sacred into our daily existence. When we embrace these virtues, we don't just reflect God's order; we become co-creators with Him in bringing His kingdom to earth.

Prudence guides us to make informed decisions relevant to our divine purpose, focusing on eternal truths over transient trends. It sharpens our vision to see the world not merely as it is but as it could be, through the lens of faith. Justice compels us to act with integrity, not just in legal matters but in all aspects of life, ensuring that our gaze remains fixed on the inherent worth of every soul. Fortitude fuels our mission, instilling in us a determination to uphold our values even when confronted with societal pressures or personal trials. Temperance, finally, offers us the mastery of self, empowering us to choose virtue over indulgence and simplicity over excess.

Engaging with these virtues propels us on the path to holiness and equips us to serve as beacons of divine light. This journey is neither solitary nor linear. It's a communal pilgrimage supported by our brothers in the Knights of Columbus, our allegiance to the Blessed Mother, and our unwavering faith in the Most Holy Trinity. Together, we foster a fraternity that lives out these virtues, embodying a living testament to the power of grace-infused moral life.

In the grand tapestry of our spiritual quest, the Cardinal Virtues are the vibrant threads that illuminate our path. They form the moral foundation upon which the edifice of our consecration is built, guiding us toward a life that echoes the divine symphony. Let us embrace these virtues wholeheartedly, allowing them to transform our hearts and minds, and in doing so, draw us ever closer to the Holy Trinity through the gentle intercession of Our Blessed Mother.

Let these virtues be our armor and shield, our guiding stars and our moral compass. As we tread this sacred journey together, may Prudence, Justice, Fortitude, and Temperance lead us to a deeper understanding and fuller participation in the divine life, ultimately culminating in our eternal union with God.

Living According to Natural Law

Every knight, bearing the mission of faith and courage, finds his path illuminated by the fundamental truths of Natural Law. This ancient compass, inscribed in the very essence of creation, guides us toward a life in harmony with God's will. Indeed, Natural Law is not merely a set of prescriptive codes; it is the divine blueprint by which the Creator fashioned the universe. To live according to Natural Law is to align oneself with the sacred order, thereby embracing the virtues that bring us closer to the Divine.

The journey of living according to Natural Law begins with an understanding of its innateness. It's written in the heart of every person, calling us to discern good from evil, justice from injustice. This inner law is universal and unchanging, transcending all cultures and times. By observing the world and reflecting on our experiences, we become aware of its precepts and how they lead to human flourishing.

Central to this quest are the cardinal virtues: prudence, justice, fortitude, and temperance. These virtues, when cultivated and practiced, enable us to live a life that mirrors the order and harmony present in the natural world. Each virtue serves as a pillar, supporting the edifice of a virtuous life.

Prudence, or wise judgment, acts as the charioteer of the virtues. It guides our decision-making, helping us to choose the right course of action in accordance with Natural Law. Prudence involves not only foresight but also a deep awareness of the present moment, a discernment that allows us to act in ways that reflect God's will. In the life of a Knight of Columbus, prudence ensures that every endeavor, whether in service or in daily life, is undertaken with wisdom and reflection.

Justice, the virtue that renders to each his due, is foundational in living according to Natural Law. It calls us to respect the rights and dignity of others, recognizing them as beings created in the image of God. Justice is not merely about legal fairness; it is about fostering relationships built on respect and love. For the Knights, embodying justice means advocating for the vulnerable, defending the truth, and promoting a culture of life and dignity.

Fortitude enables us to overcome fear and adversity, remaining steadfast in our commitment to the good. It is the virtue that propels us to persevere, especially when faced with challenges or persecution. Fortitude is crucial for the Knights of Columbus, who are often called to stand as beacons of faith in a world that may be indifferent or hostile to the Gospel. By living with courage and resilience, we honor the call of Natural Law to uphold the truth and protect the sanctity of life.

Temperance, the virtue of self-control, ensures that our desires and actions align with reason and Natural Law. It moderates our impulses and passions, guiding us to enjoy God's gifts in a balanced way. For a Knight, temperance is a daily practice that manifests in simplicity, moderation, and humility. By exercising temperance, we avoid excess and cultivate a disciplined life that reflects our commitment to God and community.

Living according to Natural Law also means recognizing the interconnectedness of all creation. It entails a profound respect for the environment, understanding that the natural world is a reflection of God's beauty and order. By caring for creation, we honor the Creator and acknowledge our role as stewards of His bounty. This ecological awareness is deeply rooted in the Knights' mission, inspiring actions that safeguard the earth for future generations.

The commitment to Natural Law is not without its challenges. The world often tempts us to deviate from these timeless principles, luring us with false promises and fleeting pleasures. Yet, the steadfast Knight stands firm, drawing strength from prayer, sacraments, and the fellowship of his brethren. In moments of doubt or weakness, the example of the Blessed Mother offers a beacon of hope and fortitude, guiding us back to the path of righteousness.

Mary, as the exemplar of obedience to God's will, embodies the perfect living of Natural Law. Her fiat, her "yes" to the divine plan, sets a precedent for us to follow. Her life, marked by humility, purity, and unwavering faith, exemplifies how to live in harmony with God's design. By consecrating ourselves to the Blessed Mother, we entrust our journey to her care, confident that she will lead us closer to the Trinity and deeper into the heart of Natural Law.

The integration of Natural Law into our lives is an ongoing process that demands vigilance and dedication. It beckons us to continually examine our actions, align our will with God's, and strive for holiness in every aspect of our lives. For the Knights of Columbus, this commitment is a testament to our faith, an outward expression of our inner conviction.

In community and brotherhood, we find the strength to uphold these principles. Together, we encourage one another, share our insights, and support each other in living out the virtues. The journey is shared, making the burden lighter and the path clearer. United in purpose, the Knights of Columbus become a living testament to the power of Natural Law, inspiring others to walk the path of virtue.

As we continue this noble calling, let us remain anchored in the truths of Natural Law. Let us embrace the cardinal virtues, draw inspiration from the Blessed Mother, and commit ourselves to a life that mirrors the divine order. In doing so, we not only fulfill our duty as Knights but also become beacons of light in a world yearning for truth and justice.

Chapter 8: Pedagogical Approaches for Knights of Columbus

In the journey of deepening one's faith, the pedagogical approaches adopted by the Knights of Columbus play a pivotal role. Teaching faith within the Order must embrace both the heart and mind, employing methods that are not only informative but transformational. By weaving allegorical narratives and epigrammatic wisdom into teachings, knights can inspire a profound understanding and love for Marian devotion and Trinitarian theology. Building community through devotional practices grounds knights in shared spiritual experiences, fostering unity and spiritual growth. Utilizing a blend of historical context, doctrinal clarity, and communal rituals, the Knights can create a vibrant, faith-filled environment that nurtures both individual and communal consecration to the Trinity through Mother Mary.

Teaching Faith within the Order

In the rich and storied tapestry of the Knights of Columbus, teaching faith emerges as a cornerstone. This sacred duty is not merely an obligation but an invitation—a calling to breathe life into the tenets of Roman Catholicism. Each Knight becomes an architect of faith, responsible for constructing bridges between doctrine and daily practice, grounding lofty theological concepts in the soil of everyday living. The pedagogy within the Order is a delicate yet dynamic endeavor that seeks to weave faith seamlessly into the fabric of knighthood.

Faith is more than an abstract notion within the ranks of the Knights of Columbus. It's a living, vibrant force that evolves and grows through teaching and mutual enlightenment. The first key to teaching faith effectively lies in understanding Christ's teachings and the Marian path to Him. To embrace faith, Knights must first grasp its essence: that faith is a journey, a perpetual pilgrimage towards greater unity with the Holy Trinity through Mother Mary.

The Order embraces a multi-faceted approach to teaching faith, wherein historical tradition and contemporary methodologies converge. Through the lens of allegory and epigram, faith is imparted not solely as a doctrine but as an enduring story—rich with metaphors that instill deeper understanding. It takes skill to transform scripture from static text to living word. In this endeavor, the figure of Mother Mary reigns supreme, serving not just as a symbol but an active guide to her Son.

A considerable emphasis is placed on scriptural exegesis. Understanding the Bible in its historical and cultural context allows Knights to extract lessons that transcend time. This approach equips

Knights to see in the Holy Scriptures not just stories of old but timeless lessons and models for faithful living. The Bible becomes not just a book to be read but a wellspring to be lived.

Inculcating faith within the Order also requires a robust engagement with the sacraments. Regular participation in the Eucharist, Confession, and the other sacraments provides tangible expressions of faith. Through sacramental living, Knights not only receive divine grace but also offer these practices as living testimony of their commitment to God. Herein lies an intersection where the sacred and the secular meet, presenting opportune moments to reinforce faith.

Meditative prayer is another essential component of teaching faith. Knights are encouraged to develop a prayer life that reflects the depth and beauty of their devotion. Reflecting on the Rosary, the Divine Office, and other Marian devotions opens channels for deep spiritual dialogue. These devotions are not merely repetitive exercises but profound acts of union with the Divine Will, drawing Knights closer to their heavenly Mother and, through her, to the Trinity.

Pedagogically, the Order employs diverse methodologies. Small group studies, encompassing scripture, apologetics, and Church traditions, foster a community of learning. This communal exploration of faith not only strengthens individual understanding but also cultivates a sense of unity and shared purpose. Knights find in these groups both a challenge to deepen their faith and a support system that underscores the fraternity's core values of charity, unity, and fraternity.

Faith is also imparted through mentorship. Senior members of the Order play a pivotal role by taking younger or less experienced Knights under their wing. This mentorship transcends mere teaching; it embodies a lived example of faith. Mentees look to their mentors as guides who demonstrate how to navigate life's challenges with a heart anchored in faith and devotion.

Visual and artistic expression further enhance the teaching of faith. The use of iconography, sacred art, and even music opens a sensory dimension to learning. Knights are encouraged to engage with these forms as they offer a way to experience and internalize the divine beauty, thus drawing their hearts and minds towards the mysteries of faith.

The role of the Blessed Mother cannot be overstated in this pedagogical journey. Mary, in her many typologies—as the New Eve, the Ark of the Covenant, the Queen of Heaven—provides endless avenues for exploring and deepening one's faith. These typologies are not just theological constructs; they are pathways that lead Knights into a more profound relationship with Mary and through her, to the Trinity.

Faith teaching within the Order is also proactive, addressing contemporary challenges faced by Knights. Issues of morality, justice, and social responsibility are explored through the lens of Catholic faith. By engaging with current events and societal issues, Knights learn to apply their faith pragmatically, making it a living and active force in the world.

The teachings within the Order amplify the significance of personal testimony. A Knight's journey of faith is incomplete without sharing his own experiences, struggles, and revelations. Personal testimony serves as a bridge connecting individual faith journeys, reinforcing the communal nature of belief and bolstering collective spiritual growth. These stories of faith contribute to a richer, more nuanced understanding of what it means to walk with Christ through Mary.

Supplementary reading and continuous learning are encouraged. Books, encyclicals, and writings by esteemed theologians become part of a Knight's ongoing education. Study reinforces knowledge but also ignites a continuous flame of curiosity and devotion. It's through this relentless pursuit of understanding that faith becomes deeply rooted in intellect and spirit alike.

The Order understands that teaching faith is a dynamic, evolving process. As times change and challenges arise, the pedagogical methods adapt, but the essence remains rooted in the timeless truths of the Roman Catholic faith and the intercession of the Blessed Mother. Knights are thus prepared not merely as passive recipients of this faith but as active torchbearers lighting the path for others.

In essence, teaching faith within the Order of the Knights of Columbus is an art and a science, blending tradition with innovation. It is a sacred dance between the heart and the mind, led by the Blessed Mother, drawing each Knight closer to the eternal embrace of the Most Holy Trinity.

Building Community through Devotional Practices

The union of hearts can only be forged through shared acts of devotion, where every knight becomes both a student and a teacher in the school of Marian love. In the brotherhood of the Knights of Columbus, this bond is not just a theoretical construct but a lived reality, deeply rooted in tradition and enlivened by practice. This section illuminates how devotional practices foster a thriving community that reflects the theological virtues of faith, hope, and charity.

A community begins to weave its intricate tapestry the moment its members engage in collective prayer. The Rosary, for instance, serves as a vital thread connecting countless souls in a melodious recounting of Christ and His Blessed Mother's life. In the same breath and bead, knights find unity, not just in recitation but in the profound silence that punctuates each mystery. This silence, rich with contemplation, deepens their individual and collective devotion. Imagine the Rosary's power magnified when a hundred knights chant in unison, the very air vibrating with sanctity.

Devotional practices must extend beyond the sanctuary, spilling into daily life like streams nurturing a blossoming garden. Simple acts such as the Angelus, prayed at dawn, noon, and dusk, stitch the rhythm of holy contemplation into the fabric of each day. When the knights gather to pray the Angelus, they not only honor the Incarnation but also renew their commitment to live in constant awareness of Mary and her divine Son.

Attending Mass collectively transforms a routine obligation into a festive celebration of divine love. Each Eucharist becomes a summit where knights encounter Christ and then descend, filled with grace, to carry Him into the world. When members of the Order come together for the Sacrifice of the Mass, they are forged into a stronger body, united in the mystical communion of saints. The communal reception of the Eucharist symbolizes and actualizes the unity of the Order in the Body of Christ.

Another cornerstone of community-building through devotional practices lies in the pilgrimages undertaken by knights. These journeys to Marian shrines and significant Catholic landmarks stand as epic narratives of faith and commitment. The laborious climb to these holy places, filled with prayer and reflection, mirrors the spiritual ascent each knight makes in his own devotional life. Upon reaching their destination, the sense of achievement and communal joy is palpable. This shared experience not only strengthens individual faith but also knits the community tighter.

The sacrament of Reconciliation provides yet another path for building community. When knights humble themselves and confess their sins, they do so not just before God but also within the presence of their faith community. This collective embrace of humility and grace creates an environment where members support one another in their spiritual journeys, fostering a communal life marked by mercy and forgiveness.

To nourish a vibrant community, knights must engage in ongoing formation through study groups dedicated to Marian texts and the writings of saints. Reading and discussing works such as "The Glories of Mary" or "True Devotion to Mary" lends wisdom and insight into the unfathomable depths of Marian spirituality. These groups become intellectual and spiritual workshops where ideas are exchanged, and hearts are set aflame with love for the Blessed Virgin.

The Feast of Our Lady of Guadalupe, the Patroness of the Americas, provides an extraordinary opportunity for communal celebration. This feast, overflowing with cultural richness and Marian devotion, allows knights to gather not only in prayer but also in fellowship. Processions, banquets, and the shared retelling of the apparition foster a sense of belonging and communal identity that transcends mere membership.

Within the Knights of Columbus, acts of service are exalted as an essential devotional practice. When knights band together to aid the needy, visit the sick, or support parish activities, their actions become a living prayer. Each charitable act is not only a reflection of Christ's love but also an opportunity for knights to support each other in their mission to live out their Marian devotion. Through service, they find and build community, extending their familial bonds beyond the confines of their meetings and liturgies.

For any community, rites of passage hold immense significance. Special ceremonies such as Marian Consecrations or Knightings serve as spiritual milestones for members. These sacramental moments, imbued with solemnity and joy, mark personal and communal growth. The presence of the Brotherhood during these rites not only underlines their importance but also reaffirms the communal commitment to the principles of charity, unity, and fraternity.

Beyond rituals, the shared creative expression of faith deepens communal bonds. Engaging in activities like creating Marian art, composing hymns, or scripting plays based on the lives of saints encourages knights to express their faith in diverse, imaginative ways. These artistic ventures offer multiple avenues for devotion, making room for each knight's unique gifts to enrich the community.

However, building a community extends beyond structured activities to embrace spontaneous acts of love and fellowship. Simple gestures like sharing a meal, offering a listening ear, or lending a hand during difficult times can profoundly impact the community's cohesion. It is in these unscheduled, often unnoticed moments that the true spirit of brotherhood reveals itself, ensuring that the communal bond remains unbroken by the vicissitudes of life.

Embracing technological advancements, the Knights of Columbus can also explore virtual gatherings for prayer and study. Online rosary groups, webinars on Marian theology, and digital retreats ensure that the flame of devotion remains alive even when physical gatherings aren't possible. These virtual spaces extend the community's reach, enabling knights to remain connected and spiritually nourished irrespective of geographical constraints.

In times of trial, such as during a global pandemic or societal unrest, the community's strength is tested. Devotional practices then become not just acts of faith but lifelines. When knights intercede together for peace, health, or resolution of conflicts, they act as pillars holding up the spiritual and emotional wellbeing of the community. Shared petitions during such times bind members closer, transforming collective hardship into a testament of their faith and unity.

In conclusion, communal devotional practices are the heartbeats that give life to the Knights of Columbus. Through shared prayer, service, study, and celebration, knights cultivate not just a community but a spiritual family. This communal journey, guided by the maternal hand of Mary, leads them ever closer to the divine mystery of the Most Holy Trinity. Each act of devotion, whether grand or humble, becomes a stitch in the ever-expanding tapestry of their Marian community, beautifully adorned with virtues and graces untold.

Chapter 9: Personal Commitment and Renewal

In the whisper of the dawn and the silence of dusk, a knight's journey finds its true essence through personal commitment and renewal. This chapter serves as an allegorical tapestry, weaving the soul's ardent quest for divine alignment. Like a pilgrim reawakening to the call of the Sacred Heart, each Knight of Columbus is invited to deepen his consecration. Just as the Blessed Mother remained steadfast at the foot of the cross, so too must the knights renew their vows with unwavering devotion. Commitment is not a mere vow, it's a living covenant, a dynamic engagement with the Holy Trinity through Mary's immaculate intercession. The path ahead may seem arduous, but with each renewed step, one finds that the Divine light becomes brighter, transforming every act of personal renewal into an act of universal love and profound faith.

The Importance of Personal Commitment

Personal commitment is the cornerstone upon which the edifice of one's spiritual life rests. In the quest for deepening one's faith through Marian consecration, personal commitment is not merely an abstract idea; it is a vital force that drives us to align our will with God's. The journey towards consecration is akin to embarking on a heroic quest, one in which every Knight of Columbus must engage with resolute determination, much like a knight in a fairy tale pledges his sword and heart to his sovereign liege.

Understanding the importance of personal commitment begins with an appreciation of its transformative power. When one commits wholeheartedly, the act itself becomes a sacred offering, an epigram of love and devotion. Personal commitment demands an allegorical shedding of one's former self, shedding layers of worldly attachments and distractions much like a snake sheds its skin. This metamorphosis allows for the birth of a new, more spiritually attuned individual.

A genuine commitment to the path of Marian consecration requires unwavering dedication. Consider the allegory of a seed planted in fertile ground; such a seed does not merely hope to grow. Instead, it strives towards the light, facing storms and unfavorable conditions with an innate drive to flourish. Similarly, a devoted Knight must nurture his spiritual seed through prayer, reflection, and action, even when the trials of life seem insurmountable.

Embarking on this sacred journey also means making daily choices that reflect one's consecration. It is in the small, ordinary actions where one's commitment is truly tested. Each decision, each act of kindness, and each moment of prayer is like a brick laid carefully in the construction of a magnificent cathedral dedicated to God and the Blessed Mother. This microcosm of commitment continually shapes and stabilizes the macrocosm of one's consecrated life.

Moreover, personal commitment in Marian consecration is not a static attribute; it is dynamic and ever-evolving. This journey requires not only making an initial vow but also repeatedly renewing one's commitment. This renewal is a rejuvenating spring, infusing fresh life into the spirit and keeping the flame of devotion ever-burning. It is through this continual renewal that one aligns ever more closely with divine will, realizing the profound depths of the soul's potential for sanctity.

This sacred commitment is also a call to spiritual warfare, an enduring battle against the forces that seek to divert us from our holy objectives. Picture a knight who stands guard at the gates of a beautiful city; his vigilance and prepared stance symbolize the spiritual alertness that personal commitment demands. The weapons are prayer, humility, courage, and unwavering faith. By standing vigil, one not only protects the sanctity of their own soul but also becomes a beacon of light for others navigating the same path.

A fully committed heart acts as a mirror reflecting God's boundless love and grace. It becomes a living testimony to the power and beauty of consecration. Each Knight of Columbus embodies a unique chapter in the unfolding story of divine love, contributing to a grand tapestry woven with acts of sincere devotion and piety.

The journey of personal commitment also necessitates community. As iron sharpens iron, so does one Knight sharpen another. Engaging in communal worship and devotional practices acts as both a reinforcement and a profound manifestation of one's commitment. This fellowship fosters an environment where individual commitments are nurtured and allowed to thrive, each knight drawing strength from the unity of purpose and faith among his brethren.

As we draw from the deep well of Marian devotion, personal commitment also invites a reverence for time-honored traditions and the timeless wisdom encapsulated in them. Through every rosary prayed, every hymn sung, and every act of charity performed, Knights of Columbus not only honor their own vows but also contribute to the living tradition that has sustained the Church throughout the ages.

In conclusion, personal commitment in the context of Marian consecration for the Knights of Columbus is an unwavering pledge to journey closer to the heart of God through the Immaculate Heart of Mary. This commitment transforms, renews, and equips us to face both the mundane and the monumental challenges of life with grace and fortitude. It is a beacon that guides us in our quest for holiness, illuminating the path as we strive to build a life marked by divine love and eternal commitment.

Steps to Renew One's Consecration

Once one has made the profound leap of consecration to the Trinity through Mother Mary, a spiritual bond is formed—like a divine tapestry weaving together mortal will and heavenly grace. This sacred commitment, however, must not fall idle. Renewal of one's consecration is a deliberate and continuous act, compelling the soul to remain vigilant and ever-devoted.

First, periodic reflection stands paramount. Just as any knight surveys the battlefield, so must one survey the landscape of their heart. Set aside time regularly—be it weekly or monthly—to examine your progress and shortcomings. Contemplate the intentions and fervor with which you initially made this sacred commitment. Was your heart ablaze with love and devotion, or were doubts clouding your way? This reflection allows for an honest appraisal, thus guiding your future spiritual endeavors.

In tandem with reflection comes the practice of reinvigorated prayer. Prayer is the lifeblood of any consecrated soul. Return to the original words of your consecration—relive them, taste them anew. Invoke Mary's intercession, that she may reignite the same ardor once felt. Consider integrating litanies, rosaries, and meditations focused on the mysteries of the Trinity and the virtues of Mary. Frequent prayer, whether in the silence of dawn or in the still of night, fortifies the bond of your consecrated soul.

Sacramentally, the Eucharist holds incomparable value. Partaking in the Holy Sacrifice of the Mass with fervent intention and receiving the Body and Blood of Christ places the soul in direct communion with divine grace. Strive to attend Mass more frequently beyond obligatory Sundays. In the Eucharist, one's consecration finds renewal and strength, for one is united intimately with the very heart of the Trinity.

Additionally, confession cannot be overlooked. Regularly engaging with the Sacrament of Reconciliation purifies the soul and renews one's divine commitment. The act of confession sheds the weight of sin, allowing the devotee to stand upright, unfettered by the chains of past transgressions. Seek the confessor's guidance in specific areas where your devotion may be waning, and take his counsel to heart.

Furthermore, extend your consecration's renewal into acts of penance and sacrifice. Offer up small sacrifices in your daily life—fasting, abstaining, or enduring a particular inconvenience for the love of God. These acts heighten spiritual awareness and commitment, drawing one closer to the sacrificial love shared by Jesus and Mary.

Community involvement also plays an essential role. Fellowship with other Knights of Columbus or devotees fosters mutual encouragement. Engaging in communal prayers, participating in Marian devotions, or discussing spiritual insights can rejuvenate one's personal commitment. The shared journey within a community adds a layer of accountability and support, reminding each soul of its pledge.

Pilgrimage, both physical and spiritual, serves as a potent method for renewing one's consecration. Visiting holy sites dedicated to the Blessed Mother or the Trinity imbues the soul with renewed purpose and inspiration. Alternatively, a spiritual pilgrimage—through meditation, extended prayer, or devotionals—can transport the heart to sacred realms, reinforcing the consecration pledge.

Reflect also on the life of Mary, model and guide of total consecration. Meditate deeply on the Joyful, Sorrowful, Glorious, and Luminous Mysteries of the Rosary. Contemplate her unwavering obedience, her silent suffering, and her eternal glory. In Mary, one discovers the archetype of perfect consecration; through her, the soul learns to navigate its own spiritual path.

Writing in a journal is yet another method of fortification. Document your thoughts, prayers, and reflections—mark the milestones of your spiritual journey. Journaling creates a tangible record of growth and areas in need of improvement. This habit fosters a deeper understanding and commitment to your vows.

Lastly, cultivate a deepening intellectual understanding of consecration. Engage with sacred texts and teachings concerning Marian devotion and the Trinity. Reading the writings of saints who have traversed the path of consecration unveils deeper layers of its profound significance. Books, sermons, and catechetical resources provide knowledge that nurtures and strengthens the soul's resolve.

In conclusion, renewing one's consecration is an ever-evolving practice—a symphony of reflection, prayer, sacrament, penance, community, pilgrimage, meditation, and study. Each step, taken with sincere heart and devoted will, draws the consecrated soul closer to the divine tapestry woven by the hands of the Trinity through Mary. And thus, in fulfilling these steps, one continually renews and rejuvenates the consecration, ensuring it remains an ever-bright beacon guiding the way to eternal union with God.

Chapter 10: The Duty of Religion

In the shimmering tapestry of our faith, the duty of religion stands as a solemn chord, echoing through the corridors of time. Knights of Columbus, valiant in their commitment, must recognize that their sworn duty transcends personal devotion and enters a realm of inevitable responsibility towards God and the Church. This sacred duty, woven into the very fabric of our being by divine mandate, calls us to live with integrity, align our daily acts with divine precepts, and serve as luminous beacons of truth in a world often shadowed by doubt. By embracing our religious responsibilities, we not only honor the covenant made with the Blessed Mother but also forge a pathway to the Trinity, reflecting the eternal light of God's love through our devotion and deeds.

Understanding Religious Duty

Within the grand tapestry of our faith, the concept of duty holds an esteemed thread, strengthening our daily lives as Knights of Columbus and faithful servants of the Blessed Mother. Religious duty, at its core, encompasses the myriad responsibilities we embrace in our dedication to God and to the teachings of the Roman Catholic Church. It is not a mere obligation; rather, it is a profound manifestation of our love and commitment to the Holy Trinity.

The exploration of religious duty begins with understanding its theological foundations. Rooted deeply in Scripture, our duties to God are illuminated through the commandments delivered to Moses and the teachings of Jesus Christ. By aligning our lives with these divine directives, we move toward sanctity. Royal knights in the kingdom of God, our duty is to uphold the spiritual and moral principles that define our very essence.

One cannot discuss religious duty without acknowledging the pivotal role of Mary, Our Blessed Mother. As the ultimate epitome of obedience and devotion, Mary's "fiat" teaches us the essence of saying "yes" to God's call. Her unwavering faith and submission to God's will serve as an unceasing beacon, guiding us towards a life of complete dedication and love for the divine.

The catechism further clarifies the practices that form the bedrock of our religious duty. Key among these are prayer, attending Mass, partaking in the sacraments, and performing acts of charity. Prayer, the soul's dialogue with God, is our daily spiritual nourishment. Through it, we open our hearts to divine grace, seeking guidance, strength, and the fortitude to fulfill our duties.

Attending Mass regularly is another cornerstone. The Eucharistic celebration is the summit of our Christian life, a mystical encounter with the living Christ. As Knights of Columbus, our participation is not passive; it is an active, heartfelt offering of ourselves to God's eternal sacrifice.

Moreover, the sacraments serve as vital channels of grace, fortifying us in our journey of faith. Confession, for example, cleanses us from sin and renews our commitment to living virtuously. Likewise, the sacrament of the Eucharist nourishes our souls, binding us more intimately to Christ and to each other within the Church.

Acts of charity—an expression of love for our neighbors—embody the corporeal essence of religious duty. Emulating the Good Samaritan, we are called to extend our hands to those in need. Service, rather than a mere act, becomes an integral part of our spiritual identity, reflecting the loving compassion of Christ.

Beyond these practices, religious duty imbues our daily lives with purpose and direction. It manifests through simple, yet profound, actions: treating others with kindness, offering patience in moments of frustration, and seeking opportunities to demonstrate God's love in the mundane tasks of life. Here, duty transcends the spiritual realm, embedding itself in our every interaction and decision.

In the context of the Knights of Columbus, religious duty takes on communal dimensions. Our brotherhood is not just a fellowship of faith but a living, breathing testament to unity, charity, and fraternity. By supporting one another in our spiritual endeavors, we fulfill our collective duty to uphold the moral and spiritual pillars of our Order.

This journey of understanding religious duty is ever-evolving. As we grow in faith, so too does our comprehension of the depths of our responsibility to God, Church, and community. Continuous spiritual formation—through study, prayer, and reflection—ensures that our understanding remains vibrant and aligned with divine wisdom.

Finally, embracing our religious duty means recognizing the profound joy and fulfillment it brings. While the path may be strewn with challenges, the rewards are divine—eternal life and the beatific vision of God. As we navigate through this chapter of our consecrated lives, let us remember that duty is not a burden, but a sacred privilege bestowed upon us by our Creator.

It is within this framework of understanding religious duty that we draw closer to realizing our ultimate purpose: to love and serve God with all our heart, soul, and mind, and to be ever faithful to the teachings of the Holy Mother Church. As the pages of this book unfold, may our hearts and minds be evermore attuned to the divine call, and may our actions reflect the unwavering loyalty of a true Knight of Columbus.

Applying Duty within Daily Life

The ethos of the Knights of Columbus, imbued with Roman Catholic faith and ardent devotion to the Blessed Mother, calls for the integration of religious duty into the fabric of daily existence. The call to serve God, live virtuously, and uphold the principles of the Church is not a mere abstract concept reserved for Sundays or holy days. Instead, it is woven into the very essence of our everyday actions, thoughts, and decisions. A Knight's life, then, becomes a continuous act of consecration, a living prayer that embodies faith in myriad ways.

In the bustling tempo of modern life, the practice of duty in daily routines may seem daunting. Yet it is in those very routines that our commitment is tested and sanctified. Whether in the echo of the morning Angelus or the silent gratitude before a meal, these small acts of devotion collectively fortify our faith. They remind us that holiness is not confined to grand gestures but often found in the quiet faithfulness to perform our duties with love and humility.

Consider the day's beginning. Rising with a prayer sets the tone for what's to come. Offer your first thoughts to God, asking for His guidance and blessing. This small but significant act of consecration can transform ordinary moments into sanctified experiences. Whether it's getting ready for work, preparing breakfast for your family, or simply moments of stillness before the day ensues, infusing these moments with intention steers the heart towards God.

Work is another sphere where duty manifests. The principle of "Ora et Labora" (Pray and Work) beckons us to perform our tasks not just as jobs but as services to God. When you approach your work with diligence and integrity, you reflect the divine purpose in labor. Every task, no matter how mundane, becomes a vessel of grace. Your attitude and commitment at work exemplify the Kingdom values, revealing a life led by divine duty.

Family life offers a profound canvas for these principles. The roles of husband, father, brother, and son come with specific responsibilities that are sacred in nature. Leading prayer at home, engaging in meaningful conversations about faith, and nurturing a loving and forgiving environment are substantial ways to apply religious duty within the familial context. Bearing witness to faith through actions provides a living catechism for your loved ones.

The community's apostolate also represents crucial ground for exercising duty. Whether through parish involvement, charity work, or simply assisting a neighbor, your active participation becomes a testament to living faith. The Knights of Columbus have a long tradition of community service, rooted in the Gospel's call to love thy neighbor. This is where duty transcends the personal sphere and joins collective effort, fostering unity and fraternity within and beyond the order.

Prayer and sacramental life are unequivocally central. Regular attendance at Mass, frequent confession, and Eucharistic adoration are pillars of duty that breathe life into spiritual discipline. They are moments of divine encounter that replenish the soul and fortify commitment. Participating actively in these sacraments aligns our earthly journey with the heavenly destiny, grounding us in divine love and mercy.

Marian devotion serves as both a foundation and a beacon. Consecration to Mary, Queen of Heaven, is not a one-time event but a continuous journey. Daily invocation of her intercession, praying the Rosary, and reflecting on her virtues provide a clear pathway to aligning our hearts with hers. This harmony with Mary draws us inexorably closer to the Holy Trinity, magnifying our duty into a divine communion.

Piety and charity should go hand in hand. True devotion inspires acts of love and kindness. These acts are expressions of faith in the tangible reality of God's presence amongst us. Helping those in need, offering a listening ear, and committing oneself to the service of others are not additional tasks but essential devotions that transform the heart and the community.

Personal reflection and continual renewal are paramount. Setting aside time each day for examination of conscience allows for an honest appraisal of one's fidelity to duty. It's in these moments of introspection that growth occurs, repentance is sought, and resolve is strengthened. This practice ensures that the duty of religion is not static but a dynamic journey towards holiness.

In conclusion, integrating religious duty into daily life is a tapestry woven with threads of prayer, work, family, community, sacraments, Marian devotion, charity, and reflection. It is the vibrant manifestation of the consecrated life lived out in the ordinary, touching the divine within the mundane. For Knights of Columbus and devotees of the Blessed Mother, this daily application of duty is a testament to unwavering faith and a beacon leading to the Most Holy Trinity through Mary.

Chapter 11: Original Consecration Prayers

In the quiet recesses of a Knight's heart, the whispers of consecration to the Blessed Trinity through Mary bloom into profound prayers. As knights, we craft these prayers as both a personal offering and a bond of fraternity, charity, and unity. Each line becomes a bridge, not just connecting us to the Holy Family, but intertwining our souls with the rich tapestry of Marian devotion. In the heart of these original consecration prayers, the essence of our dedication lies—a mirror reflecting our steadfast commitment to live in alignment with divine will. Thus, with every syllable, we consecrate not just ourselves, but our mission and the brotherhood we cherish, inviting the Blessed Mother to guide us ever closer to the heart of the Trinity.

Writing Personal Prayers of Consecration

In the sacred journey of consecration, your prayer is a vital link between your soul and the divine. Endeavoring to write your own personal prayers of consecration is to engage deeply with your faith. It's an intimate act that transcends mere words. The essence lies in your heart's yearnings and devotion towards the Holy Trinity through Mother Mary.

First, take a moment of reflection and stillness. Before you pen your prayer, ask for the Holy Spirit to inspire your thoughts and words. A prayer of consecration isn't just a formality; it's a covenant, a pouring out of your soul. Allow your spirit to be moved by the beauty of the commitment you're undertaking. Remember, each prayer is unique, echoing the personal relationship you harbor with the Divine.

When composing your prayer, start by acknowledging God's grandeur and His infinite love. Invoke the Holy Trinity, the Father, the Son, and the Holy Spirit. Your prayer's opening should be a declaration of God's majesty and your recognition of His boundless mercy and grace. For instance, "O Most Holy Trinity, I humbly bow before Thy infinite majesty, invoking Thy mercy and grace upon my unworthy soul."

Following this, transition to recognizing the Blessed Virgin Mary's unparalleled role in your consecration. She is the Mother of God, the channel through which you approach the Divine. Emphasize her virtues, her obedience, and her role as the mediator. For example, "O Blessed Virgin Mary, Mother of God, in thy immaculate heart I find refuge. Through thy virtues of holiness and obedience, guide me closer to Thy beloved Son."

Next, articulate your personal intentions and commitment. Envision the aspects of your life you wish to surrender and consecrate. Be specific and honest. This is where you pour out your soul, opening yourself entirely to God's will through Mary's intercession. An example might be, "I consecrate my heart, my thoughts, my actions, and my very being to Thee, seeking Thy guidance in every moment of my life. Empower me to live in accordance with Thy divine will."

Incorporate aspects of your role as a Knight of Columbus. Reflect upon how your commitment to charity, unity, and fraternity can be deepened through this consecration. "As a Knight of Columbus, let my actions resound with the virtues of charity, unity, and fraternity. May I serve my brothers and my community with unwavering faith, reflecting Thy holy example."

Don't forget to embody a spirit of humility and thanksgiving. As you conclude your prayer, cement your pledge with an attitude of gratitude and surrender. Trust in the Divine's perfect plan for you. A concluding example could be, "I thank Thee, O Holy Trinity, and Thee, O Blessed Mother, for accepting my humble offering. I trust in Thy infinite wisdom and surrender my fears, placing my faith entirely in Thee."

Remember, brevity or length is not as crucial as the sincerity of your prayer. Whether your prayer is long or short, what matters most is that it reflects the true sentiments of your heart. Each word should resonate with your personal experience, struggles, hopes, and faith.

As you write, you may find it helpful to incorporate elements from scripture and teachings that have deeply touched you. Biblical passages, quotes from saints, or reflections from your spiritual readings can enrich your prayer, providing it with a timeless depth and resonance.

Finally, maintain a spirit of consistency. Your consecration prayer isn't a one-time act but an ongoing commitment. Revisit and revise your prayer as you grow in your faith. Your relationship with God and Mary will deepen and evolve. Let your prayer evolve with you, continually aligning it with your spiritual journey.

In conclusion, crafting a personal prayer of consecration is a profound and beautiful act of faith. Through careful reflection, sincere intention, and heartfelt devotion, your prayer can become a living testament to your spiritual journey. As Knights of Columbus, your prayers not only uplift your soul but also illuminate your path of charity, unity, and fraternity. Through the blessed intercession of Mother Mary and the Holy Trinity's grace, may your words soar to the heavens, echoing eternal devotion and love.

Collection of Original Prayers Which Exemplify Charity, Unity and Fraternity

In the grand tapestry of our faith, the virtues of charity, unity, and fraternity form a golden thread that binds us together as Knights of Columbus. This collection of original prayers is designed to deepen these virtues within our hearts, drawing us closer to the divine love that is at the very core of our Trinity through the tender intercession of the Blessed Mother.

First, let us consider the essence of charity. Charity is not merely the act of giving but is an outpouring of divine love that compels us to act with compassion and kindness towards all. Here is a prayer to cultivate this virtue:

Prayer for Charity:

Heavenly Father,

Instill in us the spirit of true charity,

That we may give without counting the cost,

Love without expecting anything in return,

And serve with a heart full of joy.

Through the intercession of our Blessed Mother,

Help us to see the face of Christ in all we meet,

And to extend your divine mercy to everyone.

Amen.

Next, we turn our hearts to the virtue of unity. Unity is the bond that reflects the oneness of the Holy Trinity. It is the principle that binds us in a harmonious community, working together for the glory of God and the common good. Here is a prayer to deepen our sense of unity:

Prayer for Unity:

O Blessed Trinity,

Grant us the grace to be of one mind and one heart,

Reflecting your perfect unity in our community.

May our actions and words sow seeds of peace, not discord,

And may we be united in our mission to serve you.

Through the loving guidance of our Mother Mary,

Help us to be instruments of your peace,

Fostering unity in our families, parishes, and the wider world.

Amen.

Fraternity is the third pillar of our devotion. As Knights, we are called to be brothers to one another, offering support, understanding, and encouragement. It is through fraternity that we embody the love of Christ in tangible, meaningful ways. Let us pray:

Prayer for Fraternity:

Loving God,

We thank you for the gift of fraternity,

Which binds us together as brothers in Christ.

Help us to be faithful companions to one another,

Sharing in each other's joys and burdens.

Through the maternal care of the Blessed Virgin,

Guide us to be compassionate and understanding,

Reflecting your love in our everyday interactions.

Amen.

In our dedication to these virtues, we find a path toward a more profound consecration. Each prayer is a step deeper into a life that mirrors the Holy Family and the divine love that Christ showed us. The journey towards embodying charity, unity, and fraternity begins with our commitment to daily prayer.

Here, let us invoke the name of Mary, our dearest Mother, whose example of charity, unity, and fraternity inspires us. Her intercession brings our prayers to the throne of the Most High:

Consecration to Mary:

O Mary, Mother of Divine Love,

We consecrate ourselves to your Immaculate Heart.

Take us under your mantle,

And guide us to live in perfect charity,

In unwavering unity, and in true fraternity.

From your heart was born the Prince of Peace,

In whom we place our trust and our hopes.

May your presence in our lives be a beacon of divine light,

Leading us always closer to your Son,

Our Lord and Savior, Jesus Christ.

Amen.

Turning to Our Lady with these prayers, we become vessels of her love, her unity, and her fraternity. Each word spoken, each whisper of devotion, is a stitch in the fabric of a life consecrated to God through Mary. By embodying these virtues, we fulfill our role as Knights of Columbus, championing the values that fortify our faith and community.

Chapter 12: Living Out the Consecration

To live out the consecration is to weave the threads of sacred devotion into the fabric of one's daily life as a Knight of Columbus. Like a tapestry that tells a story, each day is an opportunity to reflect the divine love and grace bestowed upon us through our consecration to the Trinity via the Blessed Mother. Embrace every action, no matter how small, with the intention and heart of service, allowing the virtues of charity, unity, and fraternity to shine forth. In the morning's quiet moments and the day's bustling noise, strive to build a consistent spiritual practice that honors the consecration. By doing so, you embody the profound mystery of God's love, becoming a living testament to His glory and the tender guidance of Mary. This daily journey of faith transforms simple deeds into acts of profound significance, illustrating the symphony of a life fully dedicated to the divine will.

Daily Life as a Consecrated Knight

As the morning sun rises, casting a golden glow upon the world, a Consecrated Knight begins his day with a heart attuned to prayer. The Knight recognizes that life, filled with its many challenges and obligations, must be centered upon the Trinity through the intercession of the Blessed Mother. The first act, a whisper of gratitude and a sign of the Cross, becomes the cornerstone that sanctifies the hours to come.

Our Knight, adorned not with armor of steel but with virtues forged through devotion, embarks on a journey both ordinary and extraordinary. The day's rhythm is orchestrated by a sequence of intentional acts that transcend the mundane. Morning prayers, often recited with a rosary held firmly in calloused hands, serve as an invocation for guidance and strength. The repetitive "Hail Marys" echo like a litany of faith, binding the Knight closer to the mysteries of the Most Holy Trinity.

A Consecrated Knight understands that his duties extend beyond personal piety. Family life, work, and community engagements are viewed through the lens of his sacred promise. Whether he is a carpenter or a lawyer, his profession becomes an avenue for manifesting the love of Christ. He approaches his tasks with diligence and integrity, mindful that each action should reflect the light of his consecration. His colleagues and clients may not always understand this deeper purpose, but they feel the impact of his genuine care and unwavering principles.

During the midday, the Angelus bell may ring—a call to pause and reflect upon the Incarnation. This brief moment, rooted in tradition, is an opportunity for the Knight to reconnect with the divine mission. He might whisper the "Regina Caeli" or other Marian prayers, offering his intentions for the day. These moments of sanctified interruption remind him of his celestial patroness, Mary, whose fidelity he strives to imitate.

The Knight's dedication extends to his interactions with his fellow Knights of Columbus. Fellowship is not merely social; it is a communion of souls dedicated to a unified purpose. Meetings, service projects, and charitable works become sacred assemblies where the virtues of charity, unity, and fraternity flourish. Here, the Consecrated Knight shares his journey, offers support, and finds reinforcement in a brotherhood that mirrors the heavenly fellowship of saints.

As evening approaches, the Knight engages in an examination of conscience, reflecting on his thoughts, words, and deeds. This introspective practice is more than a routine; it is a heartfelt evaluation of how closely he has walked with God. Through this examination, the Knight seeks to purify his heart, asking for forgiveness and resolving to improve. The day might end with the rosary or other devotional prayers, sealing the hours with a final offering to the Blessed Mother.

In this daily rhythm, Sunday holds a special place—the pinnacle of the week's sanctity. Participation in the Holy Mass is, for the Consecrated Knight, the ultimate encounter with the Divine. He understands that receiving the Eucharist is both a privilege and a profound responsibility. Each Mass is a renewal of his consecration, a reaffirmation of his dedication to the Trinity through Mary. The homily, the prayers, the sacred mysteries—each aspect of the liturgy nourishes his soul, preparing him for the week ahead.

Even leisure and rest are touched by his consecration. Whether he reads spiritual classics, enjoys nature, or spends time with loved ones, he is aware that these moments are gifts from God. He seeks to engage in them with an attitude of gratitude and moderation, ensuring they do not distract from his primary mission. Leisure becomes another way to glorify God, a refreshment for the soul's journey.

True devotion, the kind that defines a Consecrated Knight, also requires a heart open to sacrifice. This sacrifice is not limited to grand gestures but is woven into the fabric of daily life. It may involve offering patience in trying situations, extending kindness to those who challenge him, or giving generously of his time and resources. These small, hidden sacrifices are the bricks that build a life of heroic virtue.

Furthermore, the Knight's interaction with the larger community is imbued with a sense of mission. Whether involved in parish activities, volunteering at local shelters, or supporting pro-life initiatives, the Knight engages with a spirit of servanthood. He sees his efforts as a continuation of Mary's fiat, a way to bring Christ into the world. These actions are not performed for recognition but as acts of love, unseen yet powerful, echoing the hidden life of the Holy Family in Nazareth.

Challenges and trials inevitably arise, yet the Consecrated Knight faces them with a steadfast heart. His consecration arms him with a faith that can move mountains and a hope that anchors the soul. He trusts in Divine Providence, understanding that every cross he bears is a share in the redemptive suffering of Christ. In moments of doubt or difficulty, he turns to Mary, the Star of the Sea, to guide him safely through the storms of life.

In quiet moments of contemplation, the Knight often finds solace in the sacred silence. These are times of spiritual renewal, where he listens for the gentle whisper of God's voice. Whether in adoration before the Blessed Sacrament or in solitary prayer at home, these moments are vital for maintaining a vibrant spiritual life. Silence becomes a sanctuary, where the Knight is reminded of his divine calling and the love that sustains him.

Ultimately, the daily life of a Consecrated Knight is a tapestry of devotion, duty, and divine love. Each day is an opportunity to deepen his relationship with the Trinity through Mary, to live out his commitment with fidelity and fervor. It is a journey that requires perseverance, a heart molded by grace, and a will fortified by faith. In every action, whether big or small, the Knight strives to honor his consecration, ever mindful of his sacred mission to reflect the light of Christ in the world.

Through this daily commitment, the Consecrated Knight becomes a beacon of hope and a witness to the transformative power of sacred devotion. His life, woven with the threads of prayer, virtue, and service, stands as a testament to the beauty of living consecrated to the Trinity through Mother Mary. In this way, he not only sanctifies his own life but also becomes a channel of grace for others, fulfilling his profound calling as a Knight of Columbus and a devoted child of the Blessed Mother.

Building a Consistent Spiritual Practice

To live out our consecration effectively, one must embrace a rhythm of consistent spiritual practice. Like the steady toll of a church bell, this practice becomes a beacon, calling you to daily devotion, reflection, and action. It is through these regular steps that a consecrated knight finds his footing in the intricate dance between duty and devotion.

Begin with an anchoring morning ritual. Before the distractions of the day arise, center your thoughts with prayer. It could be as simple as a heartfelt Hail Mary or as elaborate as reading and reflecting on a passage from the Holy Scriptures. This time allows you to align yourself with divine purpose, ensuring that the first fruits of your day are offered to God through Mary. Remember, the early morning light is a symbol of renewal and hope; let your morning prayers reflect this sentiment.

Taking this one step further, consider incorporating the Liturgy of the Hours into your daily practice. This ancient tradition offers a framework for praying at set times throughout the day, sanctifying each moment and turning your daily life into a tapestry of divine worship. The rhythm of these prayers ties your heartstrings to the grand narrative of the Church, connecting your solitary prayers to the universal heartbeat of Catholic devotion.

In moments of quiet, seek the companionship of the rosary. Each bead is a stepping stone, guiding you through the mysteries of Christ's life, death, and resurrection, while enveloped in the embrace of the Blessed Mother. The rosary, when prayed consistently, becomes a spiritual lifeline, grounding you in faith and allowing you to ponder the divine mysteries with a contemplative heart. Carry it with you always, so that when troubles arise, you can seek comfort through its gentle cadence.

Incorporate spiritual reading into your daily routine. Sacred texts, writings of the saints, and Church teachings provide nourishment for the soul. They open windows to the divine, offering wisdom and guidance. It's not just about reading, though; it's about meditative engagement with the texts. Pause to reflect on how these readings resonate with your own spiritual journey. Allow their truths to permeate your daily actions and decisions.

Consider fasting as part of your spiritual practice. While it may seem like a physical discipline, the true essence of fasting lies in spiritual renewal. It's a way to empty oneself, creating space for God's grace to fill. Regular fasting teaches self-discipline, heightens spiritual awareness, and brings clarity of purpose. It's a form of sacrifice that mirrors the life of Christ and aligns with the penitential acts of Mary.

Confession and the Eucharist are twin pillars that support a consistent spiritual practice. Regular confession cleanses the soul, offering absolution and a fresh start. It's a humbling act that brings immense spiritual growth. The Eucharist, on the other hand, is the living bread that sustains. Attending Mass and receiving Communion as often as you can ensures that Christ's presence remains the cornerstone of your daily life.

Journaling your spiritual journey can also be immensely beneficial. By putting pen to paper, you record your prayers, reflections, struggles, and triumphs. This practice not only offers a tangible way to track your progress but also becomes a precious keepsake of your spiritual walk. It provides a space for gratitude and introspection, helping you see God's hand at work in every aspect of your life.

Mentorship and community are vital. Engage with fellow knights and Marian devotees to share experiences and wisdom. Community prayers, group reflections, and discussions enrich your spiritual perspective. They create a support network that reinforces your commitments and encourages you in moments of weakness. Within this brotherhood, you're not walking your spiritual path alone; you're part of a collective pilgrimage towards holiness.

Lastly, acts of charity and service solidify your spiritual practice. Living out your consecration means embodying the virtues of charity, unity, and fraternity. Seek opportunities to serve others, especially those in need. These acts of kindness are living prayers that reflect Christ's love and Marian compassion. Through service, you bring the spiritual principles you've cultivated into tangible, impactful actions.

In conclusion, building a consistent spiritual practice is like tending a sacred garden. It requires regular care, attention, and effort. Each component—morning prayers, the Liturgy of the Hours, the rosary, spiritual reading, fasting, confession, the Eucharist, journaling, community, and service—plays a crucial role. Together, they create a harmonious life that resonates with divine purpose. Through these practices, you become ever more aligned with the heart of the Trinity, walking hand in hand with the Blessed Mother. As you continue this journey, may your spiritual practice grow ever deeper, rooted in love, faith, and unwavering devotion.

Conclusion

As we bring this book to a close, let us reflect on the profound journey we've undertaken. The sacred path of consecration to the Trinity through Mother Mary offers not just a spiritual commitment but a profound transformation of heart and soul. This consecration is a road paved with devotion, virtues, and a deeper understanding of our faith as Knights of Columbus, devotees of the Blessed Mother, and Roman Catholics.

Taking this journey, we've traversed the historical origins of Marian consecration, learning how saints and scholars have venerated Our Blessed Mother. We've delved into the rich symbology and typology of Mary in the Bible, understanding her as the New Eve, the Ark of the Covenant, and the Queen of Heaven. Each title and typology we explored illuminated Mary's unparalleled role in salvation history and her closeness to the Divine Trinity.

The Trinity itself, with its ineffable mystery and boundless love, became more accessible to us through Mary. As the pathway to the Trinity, she guides us with maternal care into a deeper relationship with the Father, the Son, and the Holy Spirit. This sacred relationship invites us into a daily, lived experience of faith that transcends mere ritual and transforms our very being. And as we understand this sacred journey, we recognize the essential role of the Knights of Columbus in promoting and living out this devotion.

Our order's commitment to Marian devotion is not just an emblematic tradition; it's a vigorous and heartfelt allegiance that shapes our actions and our community life. Through our consecration, we are called to embody virtues, practice daily devotions, and live lives that reflect the commandments and the Divine Will. Each element of this consecration molds us into better sons of the Church, brothers to one another, and servants of God's people.

Building a devotional life is not without its challenges and demands. It requires a constant renewal of commitment and an unwavering dedication to prayer and practice. Cultivating virtues, living according to natural law, and applying the commandments in our lives are foundational elements that cannot be overlooked. These are the building blocks that form the edifice of our consecrated life.

As Knights of Columbus, we have a unique pedagogical role within our communities. Teaching the faith, fostering unity, and building fraternal bonds through shared devotion are central to our mission. The principles of charity, unity, and fraternity are not mere words; they are living realities that should animate our lives and our interactions with others. We've learned that our personal commitment to consecration is a continuous process that requires intentional steps, constant renewal, and an ever-deepening love for God and Our Blessed Mother.

The duty of religion and its application in our daily lives form another crucial aspect of our consecration. Understanding religious duty and living it out with fidelity ensures that our consecration is not just a private affair but a public witness of our faith. In this way, we become beacons of light, guiding others toward truth and love.

The original prayers of consecration we've encountered and crafted, serve as personal signposts on our spiritual journey. These prayers are not just words but expressions of our deepest yearnings and commitments. They are offerings of our hearts, seeking unity with the Divine Will and the maternal intercession of Mary.

Living out the consecration in daily life as a Knight is the final, yet ongoing, step in this sacred journey. Developing a consistent spiritual practice, grounded in the precepts of our faith and the example of Mary, ensures that our consecration bears fruit. It's in the ordinary moments of our lives—our work, our interactions, our quiet prayers—that the grace of this consecration becomes manifest.

In conclusion, this journey of consecration to the Trinity through Mother Mary is both a gift and a responsibility. It calls us to a higher standard of living and a deeper dedication to our faith. The road may be demanding, but it is also filled with the promise of divine love and guidance. Let us embrace this sacred call with fervor, knowing that in Mary, we have the perfect guide, and in the Trinity, our ultimate destination. May we, as Knights of Columbus, continue to shine as examples of faith, hope, and charity, drawing ever closer to God through the loving intercession of our Blessed Mother.

Appendix A: Appendix

This appendix serves as a treasure trove, teeming with invaluable resources to deepen your understanding and practice of Marian Consecration within the framework of the Trinity. Here, we collect diverse materials, each handpicked for their spiritual richness and insight, curated specifically for the Knights of Columbus who are ardent devotees of the Blessed Mother. Expect to find recommended readings that illuminate the path of consecration, as well as prayers and hymns crafted to elevate the devout heart to new heights. Let this be your guide as you journey through a profound and transformative consecration to the Trinity through Our Lady, emboldened with fortitude and grace, ever committed to your noble calling within the Church.

Additional Resources

As we journey deeper into the spirit of consecration and delve into the profound mysteries of our faith, it is essential to equip ourselves with a repository of materials that can further enrich our understanding. The "Additional Resources" section serves as a beacon for those seeking to anchor their spiritual voyage in the fertile soil of knowledge and devotion. Here, we list various tools, literature, websites, and organizations that will aid Knights of Columbus and all devout Catholics in deepening their consecration to the Holy Trinity through Mother Mary.

First and foremost, sacred scripture is indispensable. The Holy Bible remains the most potent resource, brimming with divine revelations that shed light on both Marian devotion and the Trinity. Engaging regularly with scripture encourages a personal dialogue with God. Consider using a study Bible with commentaries that offer insights into typology and Marian doctrines to enhance your grasp of these profound theological concepts.

For those inclined towards a more structured form of study, catechism and doctrinal manuals provide a thorough foundation. The "Catechism of the Catholic Church" is an authoritative resource that explains the Church's teachings with clear, concise definitions. Paired with resources like the "Compendium of the Catechism of the Catholic Church," these texts offer a well-rounded understanding of faith, crucial for forming a heart centered on consecration.

Biographies and writings of saints who have demonstrated a deep devotion to the Blessed Mother also serve as reservoirs of wisdom and inspiration. The lives of saints such as St. Louis de Montfort, St. Maximilian Kolbe, and Pope St. John Paul II are rich tapestries woven with threads of unwavering Marian devotion. Their writings, filled with personal reflections and theological insights, can serve as guiding stars on our path toward the Holy Trinity.

Additionally, Church documents, such as papal encyclicals and apostolic letters, are significant resources. Documents like "Redemptoris Mater" and "Rosarium Virginis Mariae" broaden our understanding of the Blessed Mother's role in salvation history and her intercessory power. Engaging with these texts allows one to align more closely with the Church's teachings on Marian consecration.

In the realm of literature, books specifically focused on Marian consecration are invaluable. Works like "True Devotion to Mary" by St. Louis de Montfort and "33 Days to Morning Glory" by Fr. Michael Gaitley provide comprehensive guides on preparing for and living out one's consecration. These texts offer structured retreat-style reflections and prayers that facilitate a deeper union with Mary and the Holy Trinity.

For practical and devotional resources, prayer books and guides are essential. They offer daily prayers, litanies, novenas, and specific consecration prayers that nourish the soul. Collections such as "The Little Office of the Blessed Virgin Mary" and "Manual of Marian Devotion" consist of a treasure trove of prayers tailored to various seasons and feasts, promoting a constant state of prayer and mindfulness.

The digital age has blessed us with numerous online resources that provide immediate access to a wealth of spiritual content. Websites such as the Vatican's official page, EWTN, and Knights of Columbus' own platforms offer articles, videos, and interactive resources. Online courses and webinars, often available through Catholic institutions, also provide dynamic and engaging formats for learning.

Podcasts and YouTube channels dedicated to Marian devotion, theological discussions, and scriptural exegesis are another modern resource. Channels such as "Pints with Aquinas" and "Formed" feature content that delves into the intricacies of Marian theology and its practical applications. These platforms provide an easy and accessible way to incorporate spiritual learning into daily life.

Retreat centers and pilgrimages stand out as unique resources that offer immersive experiences. Visiting places of Marian apparitions like Lourdes, Fatima, and Guadalupe provides a tangible connection to Mary's maternal presence. Participating in spiritual retreats centered on Marian consecration can offer deep, transformative experiences that radically affirm one's commitment to the consecration journey.

For communal resources, parish-based study groups, Knights of Columbus councils, and Marian sodalities offer forums for collective learning and support. These groups foster a sense of community, providing opportunities to share insights, experiences, and prayers, thereby enhancing one's spiritual growth.

Music and hymns dedicated to Mary and the Trinity also have their place among these resources. Hymnals and CDs featuring Marian hymns, chants, and liturgical music bestow an auditory enrichment that connects the heart and mind to the divine. Participating in or listening to these musical forms can serve as acts of worship and contemplation.

Lastly, incorporating artistic expressions such as iconography and sacred art into one's devotional practice can be profoundly enriching. Traditional icons of the Blessed Mother and the Holy Trinity, whether in books, prints, or digital formats, provide visual focus points for meditation and prayer, fostering a deeper appreciation of their divine mysteries.

In conclusion, these resources are more than mere aids; they are stepping stones on a sacred journey. Each offers a unique facet of the vast spiritual landscape of Marian consecration, guiding Knights of Columbus and all faithful into a richer, fuller relationship with the Holy Trinity through our Blessed Mother. This diversified approach ensures that every seeker finds nourishment for their particular spiritual needs, drawing them ever closer to the heart of divine love.

Recommended Readings

In this enchanted journey towards a deepened understanding of Consecration to the Trinity through Mother Mary, the books and writings you delve into play a pivotal role. The literature you choose will act as guiding stars, illuminating the path, enhancing your devotion, and deepening your theological insight. The Knights of Columbus, with their devotion to the Blessed Mother and robust Roman Catholic faith, will find these readings both enriching and transformational.

Among the myriad of available texts, a few stand out for their profound impact and theological depth. First and foremost, the treatises of Saint Louis de Montfort provide an immaculate foundation on Marian consecration. His works, particularly "True Devotion to Mary," offer a timeless framework for understanding and practicing total consecration. Montfort's eloquent descriptions and fervent spirituality are unparalleled, making his writings indispensable.

For those seeking a more modern approach, the writings of Saint John Paul II are indispensable. His "Redemptoris Mater" (Mother of the Redeemer) and various encyclicals expound upon Mary's role in salvation history, making complex theological concepts accessible to the faithful. John Paul II's veneration for Our Lady and his philosophical insights combine to offer a contemporary yet deeply traditional perspective on Marian devotion.

Another essential read is the collection of works by Saint Maximilian Kolbe. Known for his intense devotion to Mary and his establishment of the Militia Immaculatae, Kolbe's writings underscore the importance of consecration to the Immaculate Heart of Mary. His texts, such as "The Kolbe Reader," compile his thoughts, letters, and sermons, which are immeasurably valuable for anyone looking to enrich their spiritual life through Marian devotion.

Beyond these saints, several Church Fathers and Doctors of the Church provide critical elucidations on Marian theology. Saint Augustine, with his profound insights in "The Confessions," gives readers an understanding of the heart wholly given to God, a heart that Marian consecration strives to emulate. Similarly, the theological treatises of Saint Thomas Aquinas in the "Summa Theologica" offer invaluable insights into the virtues and natural law, which are foundational to living a consecrated life.

Scripture, naturally, holds its supreme place among recommended readings. The Gospels, with their rich Marian typology, reveal the layers of meaning behind Mary's role. Delving into passages like the Annunciation (Luke 1:26-38), the Visitation (Luke 1:39-56), and the wedding at Cana (John 2:1-12) allows one to encounter Mary's pivotal role in salvation history and her unfailing maternal intercession.

The Old Testament, too, teems with Marian prefigurations. Genesis 3:15 sets the stage with the proto-evangelium, forecasting the defeat of the serpent by the woman and her seed. Furthermore, exploring the lives of Sarah, Esther, and Judith provides powerful allegorical and typological lenses through which to view Mary. These biblical accounts elucidate the virtues of courage, faith, and obedience that Mary exemplifies.

Church documents, such as the Catechism of the Catholic Church and apostolic letters, are also foundational texts. The Catechism offers a systematic understanding of the Church's teachings on Mary and her role in the divine plan. Apostolic letters like "Marialis Cultus" by Pope Paul VI enrich one's appreciation of Marian feasts and devotions, providing liturgical and historical contexts that deepen one's spiritual life.

For more practical applications, numerous devotionals and prayer books cater specifically to Marian consecration. "33 Days to Morning Glory" by Father Michael Gaitley is a popular contemporary guide that walks readers through a Marian consecration journey with reflections from saints such as Maximilian Kolbe, Mother Teresa, and John Paul II. This book's step-by-step approach makes the profound process of consecration accessible and manageable.

Moreover, the "Glories of Mary" by Saint Alphonsus Liguori is a cherished devotional text that explores the various titles and roles attributed to Mary, along with rich meditations and prayers that can enhance personal consecration. Liguori's deep passion for Mary shines through each page, inspiring readers to deepen their love and commitment to the Blessed Mother.

The suggested readings are not limited to ancient or strictly religious texts. Modern Catholic authors have also made significant contributions to the understanding of Mary and consecration. Works by Scott Hahn, like "Hail, Holy Queen," provide a scholarly yet approachable examination of Marian doctrines and devotions, making them accessible to today's readers. Hahn's background as a convert and theologian offers unique insights that resonate with modern devotees.

Additionally, encyclicals and pastoral letters from the wider Magisterium offer fresh perspectives and reiterations of traditional teachings, helping to situate Marian devotion within the broader scope of Roman Catholicism. These documents serve as touchstones for continuity and renewal within the Church's living tradition.

For those inclined towards literary and poetic explorations, Dante's "Divine Comedy," especially the "Paradiso," offers a sublime depiction of Mary's role in the heavenly realm. C.S. Lewis' "The Great Divorce" and G.K. Chesterton's "The Ballad of the White Horse" also include beautiful Marian reflections that blend fiction with profound theological insights.

In addition to these written works, Knights of Columbus members would benefit greatly from participating in Marian conferences, retreats, and seminars. Engaging with live speakers and fellow devotees enriches one's understanding and provides opportunities for communal growth. Recorded talks and video lectures from noted Marian theologians and speakers also serve as valuable resources.

Lastly, personal journals and writings fostered through prayer and reflection can't be overlooked. Keeping a consecration journal, jotting down insights, prayers, and personal reflections can be a profound way to engage with and internalize the teachings and practices of Marian devotion. This practice not only deepens one's spiritual life but also creates a personal testament to the transformative power of consecration.

In sum, the recommended readings serve as a treasury of wisdom, guiding the dedicated Knights of Columbus and devoted Roman Catholics towards a richer, fuller devotion to Mary and, through her, to the Holy Trinity. By immersing yourselves in these texts, you partake in a tradition that spans millennia, and in doing so, you step ever closer to the divine mystery that Mary so perfectly embodies and reveals.

Prayers and Hymns for Devotion

Within the timeless traditions of the Knights of Columbus, prayer and hymnody hold a cherished place. They are not mere utterances or melodies; they are the lifeblood of devotion, binding us ever closer to the Most Holy Trinity through the intercession of the Blessed Mother. This section provides a compendium of prayers and hymns that have been instrumental in cultivating spiritual depth and commitment among the faithful.

The Significance of Prayers: In the realm of Marian devotion, prayer becomes the conduit through which we express our innermost desires, hopes, and gratitude. For the Knights, these prayers are especially significant. They serve as a means to consecrate one's life and work to the service of God, through the guidance and maternal care of Mary. Hymns and prayers, thus, form the bedrock upon which one's spiritual edifice is built.

Morning Prayers:

- Hail Mary - "Hail Mary, full of grace, the Lord is with thee. Blessed art thou amongst women and blessed is the fruit of thy womb, Jesus. Holy Mary, Mother of God, pray for us sinners, now and at the hour of our death. Amen."
- Morning Offering - "O Jesus, through the Immaculate Heart of Mary, I offer you my prayers, works, joys and sufferings of this day, for all the intentions of your Sacred Heart, in union with the Holy Sacrifice of the Mass throughout the world, in reparation for my sins, for the intentions of all my relatives and friends and, in particular, for the intentions of the Holy Father. Amen."

These opening orisons invite us to start our day with purpose and sanctity, looking through Mary to the face of Christ, dedicating all our actions to the sublime cause of divine love and righteousness.

Evening Prayers: As night approaches, we wrap our day in the warmth of Mary's mantle through evening prayers. These prayers provide a moment of reflection and thanksgiving, allowing us to recount the blessings, seek forgiveness for our failings, and rest in the comfort of Mary's ceaseless intercession.

- Salve Regina (Hail, Holy Queen) - "Hail, Holy Queen, Mother of Mercy, our life, our sweetness, and our hope. To thee do we cry, poor banished children of Eve. To thee do we send up our sighs, mourning and weeping in this valley of tears. Turn then, most gracious Advocate, thine eyes of mercy toward us, and after this, our exile, show unto us the blessed fruit of thy womb, Jesus. O clement, O loving, O sweet Virgin Mary!"
- Examination of Conscience - "My God, I thank you for all the graces you have given me this day. I ask your pardon for any sins I have committed today and resolve, with your help, to avoid these faults as much as possible in the future. Amen."

These vesper orisons allow us to close our day in peace, fortified by the knowledge that our loving Mother has heard our pleas and petitions.

Meditative Hymns: Among the Knights, hymns sung in communal devotion elevate the spirit and unify the group in shared purpose. The act of singing together provides a profound sense of fraternity and strengthens our communal bond under the mantle of the Blessed Virgin. Consider these:

1. Immaculate Mary - "Immaculate Mary, thy praises we sing; Who reignest in splendor with Jesus our King. Ave, Ave, Ave Maria! Ave, Ave, Maria!"

2. Hail, Holy Queen - "Hail, holy Queen enthroned above, O Maria! Hail, Mother of mercy and of love, O Maria! Triumph all ye cherubim, Sing with us, ye seraphim! Heaven and earth resound the hymn: Salve, Salve, Salve Regina!"

Singing these hymns provides not merely a form of worship, but a means to contemplate the profound mysteries of our faith. Each note echoes our love and devotion, lifting our spirits toward the heavens.

Selected Prayers for Special Occasions: Throughout the liturgical year, there are moments demanding special devotions and prayers, particularly during Marian feast days or communal gatherings. Some prayers particularly cherished by the Knights of Columbus include:

- Prayer to Our Lady of Guadalupe - "Our Lady of Guadalupe, Mystical Rose, make intercession for Holy Church, protect the sovereign Pontiff, help all those who invoke thee in their necessities, and since thou art the ever Virgin Mary and Mother of the true God, obtain for us from thy most holy Son the grace of keeping our faith, sweet hope in the midst of the bitterness of life, burning charity, and the precious gift of final perseverance. Amen."
- Memorare - "Remember, O most gracious Virgin Mary, that never was it known that anyone who fled to thy protection, implored thy help, or sought thy intercession was left unaided. Inspired by this confidence, I fly unto thee, O Virgin of virgins, my Mother; to thee do I come, before thee I stand, sinful and sorrowful. O Mother of the Word Incarnate, despise not my petitions, but in thy mercy hear and answer me. Amen."

These prayers profoundly express our reliance on Mary's intercession, reflecting a communal and individual dependence on her maternal love.

Devotional Practices: Alongside verbal prayers and hymns, the Knights find great spiritual edification in the Rosary. The rhythmic repetition of the Hail Mary, coupled with the meditative contemplation of the mysteries, roots us deeply in the life and sacrifice of Christ through Mary. It's a discipline of the soul, a spiritual chain linking heaven to earth.

Moreover, special hymns such as the Regina Caeli during the Easter season, not only lift our spirits but also remind us of the joyous victory over sin and death by Christ. In Advent, the soulful strains of O Come, O Come, Emmanuel echo our longing for the coming Savior, a hope embodied perfectly in the Virgin Mother.

To sustain one's devotion, it's beneficial to keep a personal prayer journal – jotting down reflections, inspirations, and answered prayers. This practice strengthens our spiritual journey and provides a documented testament to God's work in our lives through Mary.

In the quiet solitude of personal prayer or the vibrant community of sung worship, the Knights of Columbus find both solace and